WITH-IN-SIGHT

A poetry collection by
Jeffrey Sandberg

Written from February 2017-May 2019

"The saddest thing is dying with your song still inside you"
- Brian Gianelli

First published via Kindle Direct Publishing

ISBN:9781099473579

The author can be contacted at:
jeffdbsandberg@outlook.com

Or by dinosaur mail:
106-6660 Elliott St.
Vancouver BC, Canada
V5S 2M7

Contents

Christian Discipleship..8
Rider in the Storm...9
Courage...10
Defeat..11
Discipleship..12
Inner Battle...13
PEOPLE OF THE BOOK.....................................14
People of the Book..14
Inscriptions...15
Locked...17
O, Bright Lord!...18
Polymaths..19
Signs of the Truth...20
Sky-River...21
Teacher...22
The Conduit...23
The Mountain...24
The Truth..25
Temple Death Note..26
A Question of Paradise..27
Only Man..28
Philosophy of Little Pills......................................29
Proselytism...30
Eve..31
That Day..32
Atrophy...33
Millennium..35
Names: in the book of life......................................36
Circuit Breakers..37
Despair..40
Gifts..41
Messiah the Leader...42
A knife and a storm..43
Disciple Finery...44

Availing of Christ...45
Harmony...46
Invisible Works..47
Agencies..48
Ascendance (Rising)...49
Sparrows in Three..50
Celestial Mechanics..51
Stars...52
Epiphany...54
Poet's Process..56
Stars II...57
Scorn of the Preacher...58
Dreamless..59
Forces...60
Knowledge..61
Epiphany Part 2: Failure.......................................62
Storm Authority...63
The Forest..64
Memory...65
Childhood..66
Elegy of Timelessness..67
Memorial...68
Siblings...69
Sisterly Potential...70
Sparrows - Short Version......................................71
Thoughts..72
Saudade...74
Fault-lines...75
Heart: Deathlessness..77
HEAT 78
Torment/Restraint..79
Bindings..80
OCD Heartful...81
The Crescent Heron..82
Our World Was...83

Aimless..84
Aimless I: Sea..85
Aimless II: Heaven..86
Aimless III: Earth..88
Aimless IV: Sun...89
Songs of Hope...90
In the Place of Mourning..91
Katie...92
Mercy's Parameters..94
Resonance...96
Watcher's Love..97
Eternal – the Mountain..99
Katie, Sarah, 2..101
The Living...103
Where the Birds Fly..104
Hope...106
Two Sparrows in the Sun..107
End of a Chapter...108
Zero-Point Strife..109
Kingdom Girl...110
Kingdom Girl I...111
Kingdom Girl 2 – The Singer..112
Kingdom Girl 3...113
Kingdom Girl IV..114
Kingdom Girl V...116
Kingdom Girl 6(VI): A Cage...117
Romantic Poems 118
The Moabitess..119
Nadia..120
Red..122
Solomon's Daughter...123
Lady, Absent...124
She Was Not Waiting..125
Defiance...126
Hoops and Hopes..127

Sebastian and Whimsy..128

Sebastian...129

Sebastian II..130

The Bear that Speaks...131

Integrity..132

Tinfoil...133

Elven Spirituality...135

Darkness..136

Authority of Darkness..137

Big Pharma...138

Chambers..139

Desolation...141

Grief..142

Opacity..143

The One Perishing...144

Witness..145

Ambulance..146

Hallways..147

Humanity Bound...148

I'm Sorry...149

Roaring..150

Purpose..151

The Flies of Gehenna..152

Devouring..153

The Peril..154

Crosses..155

Tides..156

Dedication: to Jenny,
my faithful sister
in a two fold sense(that matters most)

and Katie and Sarah, three-versed
That is to say: blood, love, and triplet-power

and Jeremy
for "dreaming beneath galaxies"

"Love...is the strongest bond of union"

Christian Discipleship

Of Christ and Christian discipleship.

"See the constellation from the stars."
- P. Dyck

Another way of saying this is "See the forest from the trees."

Rider in the Storm

Within sight of the mountain
A cautionary banner rages on a dead wind
All along the proudly law-plumed walls
To an end – to a hoped for means

-Open ones heart and mind-

What is more severe than curses in high places?
Than the justice in time to the mirrored align
                of Hezekiah's judicial fee
The fig in Josiah's hand set to Eden's memory
                across the Euphrates and west toward the sea
Dead kings sigh by tomb honor text in hearts of scriptural unrest
Citing the inciting of the blood in their dread
A vicious callosity, that turns an ear towards many taunts
Threading implications of the thrill of modern superlative
By reveals of pearly tongues

One thief sighted by sorrow diadems to rule over all
By a gold-hearted lily field's call
No ashes from them
nor dusty-crowned men could relinquish
In fears broken off by dying stems
Long whispered truth discovered
                in the song of Naomi's tears
Titus' arm will never break
                for youthful aspiration an upwards call appeals
Lauding gifts in hand from one serene dove after another

-Shut one's eyes and ears-

For there are slavering tongued wolves at the door
Shouting over the wailing joys of hypocrisy
So the hollow-eyed refuse his hand
To an end – to a final truth

The ruins of cities that could never fall
Never to be avenged – Above all
A deadly exquisite silence rests in blinding patterned petals – flee
To alight in the heavens
By a gold-hearted lily field's call.

Courage

During the adversary's game of sitting on thrones
Languishing in mirrored, unexpected rooms
I in image arrayed in armored regalia of verse
And scratched into my metal by metal claw
In distorted mirror there is a graven word
A word on my burnished silver shield
"Marked", it says, in clever garbled tongues
Or, one to be hated worse
To be a target of certain pale pain in future breath
Perhaps in some fiery, heathen death
My heart beats hard under godly duress
That I will survive one permission, one of many
To be put to the test
Am I now trapped, or am I going blind?

To that unhappy tyrant
One can say: "You are your own pawn
Unable to defend against simple humility"
But what is like the words upon the burnished shield?
They are unclear, like the ribbon of sunlight
shimmering on silver ocean's field
As true light in true mirror reflects
"Marked" in garrulous etchings
"for survival"
it adds, at a glance
In high angelic script
And in deja vu or mirage reminders:
"Do not fear, be courageous
Fear no one but the One"

Defeat

"Though all the earth may yield
Not I," he declared in his heart's tent
A battle decisively fought to fierce end.

This is the terror of corners and small spaces
Agonies born inside eggs of fear
Where the bleak, open heart tells of an unfolding
deception. Requiring a deciever
He could not look above it, despite heaven's abundance
Bursting with sapphires, armies
and ocean-bright flowers and music
These are only memories.

He was coated in ashes and dust flaked from burning skin
Cornered and trapped, in vivid delays
His shouts are a lukewarm rebuttal
to the heirarchies of taunters at the edge,
the precipice of this vertical, insane abyss
From which the conflict of screams breaks the ears
of their writhing audience, and decomposes
into bitter storms of blood, fire, and clouds of dust.

The verse is of no use here.
Those who watch, versed,
will find their righteousness.

Discipleship

Led by the candle of hope
There are rough diamonds matched
To the cornerstone in perfect tranquil state
By principled command of it's marvelous refractions

The way of command without being commanded
Command of the azurean armies
Command of the broken constellation
Command of the unending door

Truth and salvation mingled together at the gate
Born by Christ's unparalleled veracity
creation within creation's mind
The keeping tranquil vision of incensed silence

The same ancient mastery of that mind
coursing through the stars
One million seeds, one grain of sand
Each precious to his grace fueled hand

Who has no place in the temple grounds
In these days of sundering
Calamity of fire, song, and smoke
Lead to spirit, to the candle of hope

We are tempered in the forge of that hope

Inner Battle

Unending,
unendurable fiery taunt
spoken in secrecy
within gathering clouds vaunt
Frogs croaks adding to the madness
in the ocher-hued air

The coming wind is inspired
And just like my failing eyes
The lotus spreads its seed and dies
Belittled petals droop, tired
touched by the gravity
of many sins behind

Now churning over ocher abbey spire
to churchbells tolling time
To an age before the tall statues of deified men
Called the bellowing monsters in stormy rise
A creed in lingering music born again
To sword, wrath and flowers burned in ovens

Against the figurehead's impunity,
lightning wracks the earth
with forked and threshing laser beams of boiling hate
Within the abbey's ornate hall and hearth
The candles are immaculately kept, knowing
Now, the hour is late

Many thunders
                One voice
The mouth of which is a couplet,

A cold sarcophagus
                and the crypt above

That the spirit, unyielding, is stultified
                As the flesh rots

Inquiry of Keepers:
PEOPLE OF THE BOOK

They stood beneath the black wrathful arch of some false idol
Mortal harrowing journey now resting with God
Dreaming carried ever, ever on *in their letters and names*

Skyward held and dazzling electric forms
Scores soared beyond all pain in pain-forged storms
Pyre and stake tells the successes of the snake, *the text is burned*

Witness of the sky kissing the sea's face with weeping rain
A remembrance, all companies of hostility pointing blame
Nightmares ensared the throng, *the text is framed*

A pragmatic art to place such heirarchy in man's sight
Before anyone knew, they saw something glow amiss in the Book
and tapestries of subtle shifting witness in white light clouds forsook, *the word calls*

The same pattern was how a sword's length is measured by the span
A permanent distinction between a man's Vetruvian hand
and war, blood, the pain of new nations and unconquered land, *the Book is boundless*

The passage of seasons revealed care in the way prophecy rhymes
With events witnessed by the wise, and their fight for hearts and minds
Smoke quietly ascending from the distant call of deliverance, *the words shake*

Observers kept a sanity to the ways the waters foam and ripple
Cradled before the strong whispers of angel, sky and mirror rain
All within the spring-time tossed by the morning light, *upon the glorious page*

What kind of person would make things with such love?
Now they knew what Satan had tried to seize
And only the false dreamed doctrines of hell, *the book will be redeemed*

Their thoughts, though deep
and heavy, bore a love
That by love itself was approved, *and on the open page*

Inscriptions
from the death of the apostles, Constantine, to the modern day; of the churches
of Christendom

Like a pitcher full of the Milky Way
Eyes stir white liquid light from heaven
Distilled with a perfect sense of clean wonder
like the virtue in a glass of wine.
Now hurry, now drink
This cup of grace
This burning true emotion
This solvent to the cavernous inquiry
Of wonders in creation moved by a dove.

Priests were drunk on this perilous grace.
Where sleepless eyes deprive them
Moon casts its heavy gloam against them from above
Coloring particles of bloody water as the mirrored stars
Bear the same radiance that spreads its shine to their feet
Making known severe evils.
Amidst sanctuary interiors they feed on scribe's leaven
Questions by these stars are kept by queries of candles
The scholars strain to solve with a versed alchemy.

New voices cried "Recant!"
Confident in the right and wrong
Students to the math of the heart
that flutters, flies, and dreams upon
Wings of recitations in the presence
of butterflies, or frail supplications
burning with faith, as they are buried and burned
In mass graves and stakes and black pits
The concealment by the union of death with theft

Alertness on the great throne gazes
The world lets go of all that is love
One day great judgement will be voiced
Lawful end to bright wicks of unclean radiance
to final governance over it's last dying smoke
and the inscription from the new earth says
There will be a great work in our days
Never again locked away in holy temples
Amidst falsehood peace and melted wax.

15

"Throw your hood up" one brother said
"The angels are watching"
Crowns and heads of authority
Bear signs upon the brow
Diadem, jewel, cap, hood or ink
At the end it will be strength
On the last day it will be a name
Across an age's full length
The mountains are true to him above.

Locked

I understood the ravens' bickering visions today
and the judgement behind the locked gates pillared the way
It made my teeth and neurons chatter, in the glue of hate
Even my prayers were inchoate

Conflicting voices then sounded knowing horns
Where the right ear is more attentive to wisdom
my left hand deflects barrages of blasphemy
the end is to the right, brushing past death

The muses then fled, taking flight with ink
on wings I sprouted with blameless wonder
And the peril is far too great in my hand
To now take a decisive stand

So, stopping to do obeisance to the flowers
Married to other, sweeter laments
I grieve the opportunity, living at great expense
There is no meaning left in my nets.

O, Bright Lord!

The broken lyre on David's knees
was tuned precisely to the execution at Golgotha
And when death loomed over those brigands
Along with the later hermetic orders
(To nuns and bishops an effigy proven false)
A crown was lain
With no escaping pain
A pain that made bright the spirit
Is the spirit to be dreaded yet embraced?

Prayer is equal parts alchemy and aristocracy
And the ministers' words over the centuries
Were like vagrants begging for soap
Righteous merit on their faces like a badge
A great concealed voice roused them
From one end of the shining sea to the other
one for certain: Its not a closed Book, rather
It's my hand over your hand, but our hand
is on the pommel of the sword.

Polymaths

"There is trouble on the city-walls
One day never comes
Unless seized by force"
declared the soldiers in my head
So I thrust out my hand

"Trust me" – spoke the memory
he had answered, groaning as the hourglass cracked
and time like die are cast
the pillars casting shadows on his face
his wrinkles are designs of glory
and grey hairs, old signs of pricelessly bought mastery

TRUST them – he pleaded
pay no mind
to the dogs' outside
Stony calamity awaits them
by a scribe's final stroke
The spirit's transforming force will save us

THEY DREAM
Like me, I being once, in windy-pathed severity
With a heart teeming with living crystals
Beating in tune to the perilous roar of vast silence
in the yawning sky above the ziggurat
Eyes growing milky, cloudy, in the blatant secrecy

TRUST – came the demand
pay no mind
to the pandemic tirade out there
Not even the singsong voice of a sister
You once knew – you once knew
We are an unstoppable spiritual force
That cannot fail with the condemned

Signs of the Truth

Will this trespass be a letdown
A dismay to you and I
Distress that becomes harmful sighs?

Or will this be an hour in which
We find all there is
another waylaid sign?

a signal to the way out
It is in my empty mind
The need for an answer

For doubt is the stonework
Faith's key to the crucial elusive gate
Wicked reach halts upon the slamming door

Therein is a mild disaster, I must let go
Meditation on such severe power
Is an indication of valor among angels

Questions over the worldly fluency
I won't seek to endure any more
violent lies from other minds

And tho the enemy's blasphemies colored my heart
I can still hide my heart, protection
inside despairing blood cells, a virus

Don't ask me to endure any more
Unstoppable and cluttered sorrow
I will find a sign for all there is today
I know him, and I love them, my fear is real

Sky-River

River-fed,
Noah's misty, despairing eyes bled
He drank of the insight of God
Drank from the river of paradise,
Drank from the river of mighty disparity
River of a crystallized promise,
River of hope captured in organic glass
River of color that colonized the promise
of no more murder from Nineveh to New York

Leprechauns are certain not to be at the edge
(of homo superior it was said)
"We have no hope! Look at who our fathers are!"
Then they began to kill
They began to enact the spirits of war
The survivors became like crowned snowfall,
Became the certainty of those who are blessed
So with broken teeth and cloven tongues
Into east and west domains the demons fled

In midst of the overarching draconic waste
The center of nowhere was heard in canticles of ancient rime
And every military official was a tower of Jericho
Upon the soiled earth
The Catholics left one standing stone in Ireland
to carve a starbound home
(His name was William Butler Yeats)
(the poem was "The Second Coming")
Heavens synaptic nerve shut
like dopamine, toward acidic arrogance

And on the reverse of Caesar's coin is inscribed:
"Every major world event happens twice"
Thus carried on a wistful breeze
the thought of death lingered,
then let those thoughts in effort either drown
or burn

Teacher – of the Book

Teacher
There was the perplexity of sadness in your sad grin
A lifetime dealt cards to setting apart grief from sin
You entrusted me with geodes
and hidden gestures of gems and treasures
But will I know sacrifice
Will I grow when finally sanitized
My need is to burn the abhorrent thoughts
Before your precise clockhand faces the hour 'late'
Only once is one time to put out the fires

Teacher
Will I suffer utter despair
Only behind me, where my nuclear diligence fails
Or before me in the choking of all these burning grasses
All unreason and fields of distress and madness
My desperation won't end in the furnace of my plastic mind
Can you put out the fires with a dilution, a monsoon
A salvation in motionless trance, a constructive melody
Any given variable on any of your healing winds
Please, Teacher, guide me

The Conduit

I know I'll never see the sun
Yet I believe in a way beyond the fire
In song without a hope to sing

Together we will find another way thru the fire
Suffering, wracked and plagued with toxins
but still breathing, a word in the water
Joy blooms beyond the waves

Hope comes with a shout, the sun is set free
Complete in living memory, spellbound
by the holy one.

The Mountain

I locked you away in my heart
So many times
And I've killed you far too many times
To ever understand the grief of why
Soft eloquent words elucidates
This sacred, crazed sorrow
Whispers of moments where soft hands were
Carry me onward
(I couldn't bear the loss)
So I captured the starlight
In every memory I had of you
Scriptures ruptured from my mind
Vibrations of distant earthquakes under my feet
Twofold division to the conquering sovereign voice
Torn – the way meets with indecision
The root and core of decision
(I've been here so many times)
I could never choose
The empty air couldn't keep us apart
The essential eternity of you lost
somewhere in the futility of my tears
You must choose
I will keep you overhead, infinite
As I carry onward

The Truth

The flow of distinct magnificent trials
Is delayed from iron distance
And the choir's bright eyes see for miles
Through the vision of gold-cup silence
For the crowds beside the trees
This peril fuels the perception of their faith
The song, the trust, the beams
Form an answer in a final place

Temple Death Note
The Battle of Hastings meets the End

The military companies were in chiseled harmony
One for another, let the ancients
Speak, in illimitable cries
How men will contend, tire out,
and perish. But God supplies
Unlimited waking power

Blood on the field,
like wine poured out into Woden's river,
the stream that feeds Yggdrasil, Saxon's lifegiver
Gives rise to trees bearing wasteful fruits.
Like a glass cup cracked by sudden cold
the prideful gleam in their frigid eyes
forecasts finality.

Monstrous faces in the steel
Death has visitors, wasp's bite
Once is a stinging rebuke
Twice is a measured cup for Taillefer
The transgressor, and the tree uprooted
That was once shaken under unharmonious winds

Crystal stream, waters of life,
flows from the conquerer,
one king's word to all other kings,
through the watery gauntlet it built
Is an angrily withheld jar of dust. He said:
"Use your power of reason,
not just your heart."

A Question of Paradise

One with questing subtle senses
Touched with graven recognition
Can discover the question of song's delight
Find the cities doom too bright
Gaze into the peaceful sense of deliverance
Struck by embers beyond insight

Thus precedent to valley's peace before bloom
A spent eternity inspired in a single tune
Heavenly eyes, strings and deep concert
A legacy of music for tall wandering prophet
Sings to a tribute of sparks, billions flashing their calm
It is yours now, in webs of priceless bonds

Only Man

Humanity is lessening down the drain,
What perils shaped our behaviour,
What black dollars pervade our times?
Whose image are we anyway
Whose touch of wisdom is this inner calm,
Who is hanging onto the past,
And are these pearls providing the signs?

Philosophy of Little Pills

The grey youth tremble with loveless eyes
The word of hope and despair serves no longer
So they command vaguely, not to certain vacancies compare
Converse on sunny days of dark truth
Tend to natural cycles of aphorisms
Furious at the old gardens
Dull fingers pointing aimlessly at the history books
Or the coming moon. They fear
That fearsome title which causes the yearning

And on the high place the tree and brick
and the castlekeep hums with answer, mastership
and authority. Full and rich with death,
Dark with orders in language, figureless in the throne,
The crown lies at the bottom of the sea
the waves break the bitumen in the cliff
The dolphin moans, the oysters clap shut
The pearl is out of reach
For those men who fear the power of learning
Are crowned destroyers.

Proselytism

That's what they seek
Vast, raw potential
The yearnings of a world-blemished mind.

I am desperate
For all extremes of emotion and mind
Fiery container of living lament
Bearer for the text from the thousand scribes

I will call out for it
Direction above
Many from within
Higher truths found
Book-bound and
Unleavened.

You can trust me
When I take your starving hand
A wilderness' potential before you
Beyond the lines of grieving sand
There is little more profound
In this moment, you and I
Than the motions of the eternal
Being encompassed, oceanbound, divine

Eve

She found, with a vile endurance
A fault of fruit in the mistaken garden's deliverance
A bane of the cellular atomic wonder
Braved the magical furnace hearth that her daughters
bowed to. How her moon wept, creeping,
for and over crescent streetlights of the future, and how suspicion
upon the kingly harp, teaching her children lonely cloudy arts,
smoldered within her veins without stone nor star.
Blood cells teetering in the apple trees that hung, now kindling
A raw flame over her body
The alphabetic rudiments also.

And the key turns once only
Many for the prophets are certainly aware
Where that blinding weave of wind out of Judea
Curled the heat of red sand pressured under each white foot
Ten toes numbered like war horns, humble and governmental
Glassed over eyes with teachings of green dewdrops
and a special blue pupil focused there, with the hard knowledge
of the glancing over of ever youthful mankind
Want of deep stillness and cries for sailing
Murmuring beside the saving power.

A heap of broken wisdom lies
in the prisons of the man
of the thorny field that the husband tended.
And their understanding, streaking above sired mountains,
left craters and epochs in the sky.
released from the jails of tall apostle's
wonder after the storm, in bright mind,
Their clues pointing, with pitiless confidence, standing
Just as where the cherubs stood
Solitary and strong, quiet and apart
Slayers, the true sword
Godly and merciless

That Day

I had a dream in the rain
And an hour of deathful sleep
Creation within creation of itself
Portends I can at last rest
The eagle has a superior eye
An array of their kind, gather together
Winged wisdom, from Egypt to new land
Fear for the shot in the dark unknown
Vultures and men eat together
Speaking riddles of dreaming and pain

How many would believe
in the end of the world?
Can I at last rest?

I had a dream in the sun
and an hour of wrathful sleep
The feel of death for all horrible reasons
Failing God, losing love
And the crows have knowledge of this
For I have a fear of light
More than their abyssal tongue, at times
Betrayers and drunkards eat together
Virtue colors the stormy lining
With colloidal silver and white druggery

All is a dream of nations
And I can at last
Rest.

Atrophy

Walk with me, along the last chill canvassed sea
Over abuse and disease to refuge with tea
Further meet calming charm breath of fresh trees

I hope to answer only all that went right
If you deign to ask me what went awry
For that rule and ruin tastes like bad honey in grottos of night

In declaration, I see with feverish dread some
Who's grip on the steadfast had been overcome
The fear bellows dormant in their atmosphere; no stars, no sun

I was one; stripped of any a lasting song
The poisoned sky held me in colorless bonds
Crushing through me like marching wrathful dust

No one stopped me, and with
Painting false memories and wishes
Comes a question;

What would atrophy?
The dragon scorched me
and maybe my brothers.

Whose shadows scream upward
from red cities' fire belly
With horrid smoke priced as a test

As avid agents for ethereal war mustered
A heartful of the foreseen recedes,
Take a moonlight shower on the city street;

In the wake of that evil shine.
And we became whole like before,
changed, worded like gold crumbling powers,

And the mighty kings cold statues
Fell, hung by temptations tall, chains
Strung from rocky dark clouds.

And that primal daystar, the good hot sun
Baked the remaining bricks one by one
The capstone butterfly's light has newly won

Walk with me, on my last dead road
Tell me you'd have done better if sown
Among the rocks, the scathing heat of hopeless hope.

Millennium

Tonight
Under cast-iron stars
Darts the flaming harm
I want to show you the lesson
of how I learned wisdom from you, to be
Forever awake, never to stay longer than the question
The thunderclap shone this message in cathedral sand,
electric heaven and striving eye
Today, love is just more treachery
Wonder no longer, under sweeping clouds
Touch the stone, fingers of my weeping
Declared today.
I will love, live and die by you
And I will find you on the shoreline
Where your name was writ in the standing sky

Names: in the book of life

There was a wonder of the hidden fire and the distant sword
The hidden fire: the mystery of two hearts floating with the sky
And the distant sword: Master, King and Lord
Calling to know these names
Greater than any brave or quailing heart

Shame or fire or wrong
The inclination entertains the aberrant, in thought and song
But maybe angels can see electrons, and these forms of thoughts
Are confined under their duress, disregarded
For too much love; too open, too dying.

When I saw, what I saw, is kept under wise union
A vision of true peace in every place
A bliss, and constantly shouting, their birth, angelic grace
Now, hand in hand, caressing leaves and cupping sand
With tiresome notes and infinitely bright man

To trespass over one gaze, one of new love
Two climbing eyes, full of signs but omens rejecting
A week of ages over a field of white wheat stopping
and black hearts harvest, ending with the cavernous pure few
It is a lesson on how to better weakness and search love new

And I dread my own weakness
Fearing the failure at my fingertips
Straining pages with the infernal, the crippled
heart in its stunted destructive growth.
I would burn all of it for just one more
Look at the bright, insightful name

Circuit Breakers

We begin
Recalling sacred text. The anointed are unannounced
Earthly hope and disparity
The encyclopedias are mirrors. The car door shuts
Unknown and unnanounced.
Paths forged out of parking meter numbers

Ley lines, city topography
Destruction met with secrets
No stumbling blocks here
The Kingdom on the globe in power, against
Egyptians with money, magic, drugs, who built stonehenge
Same displays of elementary illicit strength

Not one known who is close
Cigarettes long before were portalesque
Distrust and confusion with a David
Matters felt wrong, what King?
It wont work that way
It wont; the hospital stands dark

Astonishment with namings
They bore names.
Glittery, starlight on a cell phone
Talk, talk to the guidance, severe harm
Beckons before the righteous ears
I cannot ever understand fully, they the human suns

Walk, wait, introduce
Never to be pressed beyond
I'm not worth to speak, there
Is fear, worry, indulgent black heart
An encounter allayed, a strong
Bright hundred manned emergency

Status and role set
I believe this passage too
Machinery mentally? Hang
Onto the King's hem
We are in for the ride of a lifetime
The Jew is borne by hosted horse

Hoofprints, thunderprints
Not many else know
Penning for sustenance, direction
The scribe, the scribe, am I one?
Emergency with so little or so much prayer
Follow them, not my false prophecy

For now they recite cords of love
Relinquished to her, my
heart is blackened, sooty.
"Have mercy on me"
For she was revulsively appalled
Unrecounted and motherly claimed

Recall the parking meters
Egypt to New York to Vancouver
The ley lines and maps of hell
The angels who saw me as I fell
Perils, powers and a watch
I will stand, emanations sought

Stop, strength by fasting
Pushups and rejected moans
Potiphar's wife and demonic strife
How escape I from men in white
The thunder strikes one, dressed
I flee, streak, and return to doom

Hop to the kingdom chirping inanities
Insane visions of agony on the TV
And the sun is broken from its power
A patterned mantra coupling earth and sky
Soothing to the heart's sighing, nalia's luster
The last motif of a long repentant dying

Then they swat with unfree hands,
invisible hailstones, an anomaly of force,
how divine a strawberry bush in this shine, I intoned
They, being systemic, know none of this
As did I in the uncertain time, a bird with broken wings
What will I become? An apple in her hand

Oceans higher than the calls of desolation
Murmur in distant places, spreading
All its message across the sleep bearing seas of rest
A partial glory and comfort, melodies
Straining upon the tree grasping wind
I may never recover.

Despair

Fatally, snowflake patterns
bury the telling groans of true despair
Breathe in the cold adversity, and tell me
Why again will I wander and ache?
Under a hand that cannot quake
and an adversary breathing corpses down my neck
/
Weather changes churn clockwise
Like the light on ancient marble
Rolling slick with the blood of doves
on gameboards. And white capstones turn
grounding swirls against the enigmatic
swirls of starless sky
/
Breathe in the adversity, once again.
Can I answer with anything for the depth of my own integrity?
(in my wandering, aching heart)
Is the whole course of this existence ruined?
(will I wake to flame or be set loose)
Can I feel redeemed with a cracked-
/
-clinking glass- value? Less value
more inanities – Drink, gulp, a spattering
Every door is a mundane portal to nowhere else
Bomb the portals, with misery and trash heaps
the magnified flashes of eyes and spectacle,
The ruin of the granite cliff face breaking.

Gifts

The gifts of repentance live
By the miracle of forgiveness
In pallid powerlessness I watched
Something living wake
In the heart of my great fire stood
The lodestar sang on the way home

The masons lay the bricks
The chapel door is hinged
The priest confused the paupers
The door swings shut
The comet swings by
Endured by the violins

Do we understand each other's books
Or whose knowledge are you gazing after for?

Messiah the Leader

Birds that see chains, eyes that flower
Unduly aggravate, kingly commiserates
to the birds that recall breath , gazes that flit, awake
In the dread of towers greater as a mystery bequeathed
An undone notion that stirs awake in lamplight wreathed
From distinct darkened life I find myself to be
So close, shadows and lies mask you from me
I shut my eyes to wait for sleep in light

A knife and a storm

There like a knife in storm of thought
Like wind cutting waves in powerlessness
An armed mind of seeking, lit by forks
Orbs merging whole-bodied mass of remorse
For I am unable to stand before the lamp of God
A pebble trail to the truth that died
Among the patches of yearning grass and sighs

Disciple Finery

You have the contempt of Hades; he spoke
The host of the same terrors
that led some in throes
On the outcroppings, falsely led here
Between river, road and luminary

It just so occurs, that in the court of high reason
Cliffs and crags take the presence of another
For it takes the presence of another
To lift someone up
Especially from ash, remembrance, and dust

Before all that, from the sparking captures
of sea to futile groaning sea
There was the demand of diamond origins
The "I", the Semitic hand, of personal power
Fingerprints writ with judgement in the hour
Touching to comprehend tongue, ear and soul
When each life each day warded off the bent answers
of any lesser prince

How subtle then, and severe the drums
Of airy Israelite trumpets
That return thoughtless lure to knowledge enduring
A clue in the command, boasting
With love's freedom, love's apparition
My life is spoken beyond, I am choking alone here
Choking on glue and cost

Battle, battle the frost, the crippling
the tribes awaiting the promised voyage
Bursting blue and unchanging like a womans eyes
Or stars and cirrus and sky and peerlessness
Only the failure of containing a gargoyle smile
Sin to each clumsy sin within
What kind of bleak safety
do your trusted ones pretend?

Availing of Christ

Avalon of the Leader
...A Crowd of Stars
A sonnet...

Among the thoughts whereof watery spheres play
Wings shadow the will of a man whose will
(must never decay)
He built starlight grottos above in cityless days before
Greater irises marking the way of unknowable doors

Those circles of intent reach the hidden form
For beyond an army of his peers
(from fearing clouds unborn)
There is fulfilling the nature of sky-graced eyes
Risen becomes severity for the divinely tried

And on his path, the wings flight and gather
Keeping with true voices the embrace of wonder
(To shine, to compass)
To plead the ringing sun growing within death
for man, by the powerful star, of holy mind's duress

And if he kept this music within you
You will know the false lamp from the true
(Should you reach past this anger and pain)
to embrace the truth with fight
You will find two birds among a throng of flames alight

Harmony

The Devil's not in the details, as they say
Spiritual things are in the details
It's where you find the illustriousness,
the majesty, the grace
and power. Harmony's tracings
on the wind, the undying letter

Alien to the crowd of starry words, one
To put together the mosaic before perishing
God's help is required
We can crack the maze
This colorful and extrusive candle of life
In the home of a soulless light
You have the contempt of heaven

Invisible Works
Thoughts on Messiah

Fisherman's knots tell stories, and nets break
The man and the white stone collude
And rise above a drowned flash of water
from moon to dark branch, shaking the twig
Where the wind became one with the life
and proselytes feasted the fruit in their error
and there was a calculated malevolence
Among the snapping teeth of their own
Don't let them in, the day's fruition is wicked.
Don't let them quake your heart

Agencies

I saw with faulty eyes, here was a vile crow on the pier
that vanished before the extended watch of God.
Or just a raven, nothing more, perhaps my sight misleads.
Yet it reminds me, to abhor the evil path, the cruel road
Like turning over a dirt-mound mind that spent too long in the pit
Causing a loss of my voice to begin again,
before the blinding purity owned by graceful stars
and standing fishers of men. I confess and will not resist them.

Those two canvases and tapestries of once vague visions
White and red, coursing through the wings of the black world,
A war of worlds; the crowlike motions towards
divining trespass touching the same collapsing spiritual harm
An alarm like a hearth in wild places: "Look at him! It's not that way!"
Coupled to a thunderclap; "here, in this gaze. Among the lilies.
In sight of the sparrows. The wisdom. There's peace."
A simpleness behind no darkness, and the power to purge.

So tell yourself of the purity, and I will meet you, unrighteous
With foolish blatant words to spell out the seeming end
I'll bet all those who gaze or glimpse truly know the futility
There is forgiveness in hammer and nail
Consider this as a note from a slain one in the last days
I would plead once in faith: Please don't forget I tried.
For now I walk dead, bearing only a drink offering, with trembling
A cupbearer bearing little cause for hope, both cold and hot.
Hoping for the leaves, the healing, the spirit that mends.

Ascendance (Rising)

A powerful star, a powerful star!
Who peaceful lit a path for blackened feet
and sundered, and smoked, an agony
With the pale glimmer dying in the alien gods, in their eyelessness
        the teraphim idols seeing the unknowable
        distance.

A clamor so great, a din in the void
and blackest dense darkness preserving this:
Austerity! Knowledge beyond, and far off, in-between, within
clouded stars, high above Nazareth, and a pomegranate world, for the grave
        turning against the full moon
        To rise,

        As a stone, cut, and swords crumbled to dust, elysian,
        against the mettle of immortal mind
        A dewdrop on a lily here in the astrologer's ignorant clutch

        And the faithful knew the letter from the Law.

Sparrows in Three

Sparrows, being heavenly
Know clover luck tricks
They are too spritely
To suffer nor fester
With the worms they devour
For man, a weak leaf lifted hand
Is one leaf weak lifted wind
As a wind mourns distant
And a sparrow wing is outgrown
by the coming land
Accounted to ancient ire
Beyond a bubonic stroke
All 'round the sad shallow
subtle shifting powers of sleep
Awaken at the dawn as we
Must Be.

Celestial Mechanics

Celestial mechanisms.

"The seat of the soul is where the inner
and outer world meet, and where they
overlap, it is in every part of the
overlap." - Novalis

Stars

Distinct from heavy handed order, the wind
Led me down the mountain
to the river, seeking thought
beyond Solomon, through doors
without hinges
Wondrous journey of mortal fear

One gaze at first I saw
the morning one, alone
But I sought the tune of the millions
And myriads did ring, the wind was still
Hushed, composed
I hear them still

To the wind they say Try – try hard, but
Don't blow where solitary cares collapsed
Under aquatic miseries
Our beams of great truth
open into mountainous regions
of sheep and animal skins

For we, we are fond
Of unseen origins
Our shine ushers man's heavy lament
From one age to the next
A scriptural sentiment, to us
Is a fallout full of butterflies

For during the dark night of King David's soul
His open fever led to a mighty wind, crashing
above trees, daffodils, and our hearts alight
With right, rite and righteousness, our eyes open
Beyond the point where the philosophers
committed murder with their sciences

We heard, when Gabriel likened the righteous to us
And burned ever more constant;
Pleiades, Kesil, bound, like clockwork
to those of us with no set course
harmed secretly
by the unnamed defilement of astrologers

Some of us, although unseen,
are nebulous to the extreme,
to the point of insanity
Others are single, focused
like the eye of a Christlike disciple;
and at face value, each of us has a name

Energies unbelieved,
a man's heart in lieu of one of our brothers
Is an impotent passion, a contrived glory
We are content to stand, unsated, on our own
Advising those who traverse earthly prisons
Giving hope to those who perceive our vision

Cruel daylight opens like the lion's maw to consume us
The day is full of crow-captioned hypocrisies
knowing nothing of our gambled musings
of the silver eyes governance
above a meeting place, a trance of light bulbs,
Bright and flowing like cups of honey

In such trance upright man is condemned to a sudden wrath
Voiced in futility, observed in vain ritual of breath
Breath after breath, until all substance is past
With one life's gaze at our dwelling, a homage in fleeting wonder
Our pristine home, that he invades with many dreams
Knowledge imperilled by the failing wind

But we, who are lustrous in thought
Suffer time.
In echoes of our loneliness, mountains
will ascend. Rivers
will abide impermanence.

Epiphany

White galleys flow across the sea
        to the mountains
proud sentinels of never wilting
        earthen might
Tall one crowned by the dream-banisher,
        the molten disc
That keeps the door behind them sealed.
From what nightmare comes this engulfing smoke and ash?
The sky becomes as fire red sand
        Bright beacon of fear
            to a simple-eyed man

So another ones eyes seek
        All the fullness of darkness' hour
Stranded like dull-lit pearls
        The clouds chase the moon they shattered
Just like pottery, or broken government
        And sunlight stewards eye was closed
The tall black sentinels still guard the door
        Sealed- Sealed- Sealed away
They feel the loud clamber of water poured over powdered bones
        Inside their cavernous bellies,
        their gaping mouths
No one spared them the pain of weeping or indigestion
        Now they sleep
Ashes settled on their garments
Choking
        choking
            choking
Birds are crying for relief
The mice are hungering, going blind

What is revealed
By meditating in this emptied chamber?
Enter the third observer
To act as an evil
Little human; deviser, pragmatist, endurer
In the same way King David gazed
at blood rivers in his veined arm
feeding power to his hand
(An artifice of fearful inspiration
for man to write Vetruvian man)

His reach exceeds his grasp, and his grasp exceeds his nerve
Yet man grasps at straws, unknowing of power

The keys shake
The guardians do not wake
The sun has frozen in the sea
The moon is covered over like a leprous wound
No sound, pure secrecy, the ground quakes
the long days of reigning kings tumble
One over another like falling apples

Thoughts of the key turning once, just once
The way is open, unsealed.

   Something changed
   in the structure of the stones within time
   For divine warning is simultaneously
   a commanding whisper and a pleading shout

But he hears nothing over all the white silence
Gulls call from the guardian's feet, aloof
capturing the still life of this new precipice
A solemn reminder
In their throaty cries

Poet's Process

Vividity- step One
For poet's proclivity towards soul heart entanglements
and desperate affections seeking that of wholeness
The apparatus of distinct diction, living in inspiration
Is the same as listening for the tuning fork struck upon a star
Loosing by tone those impoverished, groping believers
(My thoughts, released by cuts of savage seppuku honor)

Inspiration – step Two
Or now bells tolling beyond, ahead of the proselyte oceans
Insane worship spreading miles of darkness at Mass
Thunder growls on the mind's borders like a nation's alarm
Like criminals under law speaking in tongues
Speaking with misshapen, goat like words

Commands – step Three
now goads to the prophecy top pen and contemplation
Perhaps be seeing like Janus, the two faced guardian
Or the Apostle Paul, looking ahead, not behind at crimes
Angels see, turning away to sigh

Obedience – step Four
Followed by threats of trivial longing
Under deepening duress
The rainwater soaks

Blessing – step Five
The threefold emphasis of spirit
Tirelessly gives way to a kind of baptismal pain

Listen – Finale
To unchained voices in heaven

Stars II

Look! Nightly terrors meet under their laughter
They are muses blind to your sin
The shaking of heavenly powers felled their paradox pillars
Astrologers will search Orion's belt for triune god hints
It is a wasteful peril to gaze at their delights among earth's kin

"Let us burn" they whisper, only to the alone
And their light turns into sulfurous gaping doors
A view to the coming of the origin of angel's hate lies
In what was heard in the iniquity of linguistic changes formed
by scattered incense fires and preachers of Babel's lore

Their spirit puts faith in the wicked
The same spirit of defiance in inane forces
Caught up over the centuries to the modern age infected
They are the same ones that saw the Flood of earth's last course
The same variables in stars, satellites, planes,
and other watcher's frequencies covertly recited
In distant time church-spires surveyed the same forbidden vistas
With structural integrity lacking without the constellations

Dangerous gazes into the scripture by them
Are soon there in shifting shadows
And in the shadow of their fear, lessons
Do not examine the text too close then
There are baffling treasuries of overwrought plans by the host

Eastern beliefs in God are controlled in their shade
Remember the daylight before occult thoughts pervade
How the colony of light cast by your watchface fade
In reflections, purveyance, or dappled verdant grief
born by the sighing forest pines in green
Chasing away their thoughts on the day and woodland lane

But inside the ice cold casket of your own belief's kind
You are also desired by their faith in you, though unheeded
Do not become blind in this forest
because of the wild greed
for understanding in your bloodied need
The answers are shining on the prophetic horizon, and in time
Finally undone by their own seductive lights
You will see the grievances of these comely stars finally burn out.

Scorn of the Preacher

I was bound once, in dark chains deserving
A thing like a cracked millstone cast into the sea
Falling, an octopus without legs, falling
Dead ashore with spilled intestines in tenuous reality
We, though together, are not so alone, so raise your goblet
I too can count the stars in their array
Can count flowers gracefully arranged
Can feel the freedom in their ways
Can trace the fixed cosmic leagues unknowing
from star to bewildered star

As revelers they gambled that mortal conceit away
Awake and confused by a promise in the full scorn of wine
Divinely confirmed as drunk since the time of Babylonian reign
Uncomprehended glass fuller tips to keep at bay such insight
Perhaps to life in perpetual mourning, like the sadness of those moons
That watchfully apprehend the heavy happiness of heaven
Like a partaking of blood, or the spiritual war outside
mystic vapors which rise for the tongue and warn the heart
Murmuring without restraint all of the power in love and art

This is a sour path, tasted to know shaken states of waking
How unsafe it is far from smoking slumbers of the druggery in your head
In nightmares number storming the battlements of the mind
The turning of the shadow creeps, descending from the horizon
rising above the sea, choking the stars to death
Where met the fear struck child you are, your feet dowsed in blackness
Birth of the sung heavenly mystery behind the beholders of earth's breaking
As far off cities burned with a startling lack of outcry
All this in your ruinous aims and timeless things that in dying must last

Dreamless

(Form: a 5 stanza pantoum)

You are a maker of pain
Inspirer, granter of dreams
In this long dreamless sadness
With hunted eyes, what then do you know?

Inspirer, granter of dreams
Fear between two angels, at long last
With hunted eyes, what then do you know?
After favor of lots cast

Fear between two angels, at long last
It became a conspiracy
After favor of lots cast
Masterful disaster opens the productive land

It became a conspiracy
There is still a terror in a hot vent
Masterful disaster opens the productive land
with a tired freedom along the ancient sky

There is still terror in a hot vent
In this long dreamless sadness
with a tired freedom along the ancient sky
You are a maker of pain

Forces

"Forces are broken," told the whispered spirit,
"Composed of ushered requests for a clean law
A barrier denouement, a regression
of love for an end
What does the numbered music portend?"

Shut the door, regard the lit lamp arrayed halls
How precarious sea water sings along
Thought between this forges frailty and a call
Of drift constellation above sand
Light caught jewels that touch upon the hand

Open the door, lead eyes from natural law
A command from well-watered places beckons
A barrier denouement, love for endings
Heaven's gifts blow satellites thru mists
belonging to sun mystery's tryst

The ocean trained us, he saved us. Never once
To visit ancient goddess' bloom, nor to bow
To anything, anyone substanced like the moon
Go ahead now, stare
See the constellation from the stars

Knowledge

I know less now than I ever did
I think I'll talk to my enemies
I think I'm broken under the rain
Maybe I'll dream up another way to be free
Ideals raining down
Just the temporal golden rays of sun
The non-ideal motion is run of the mill
I think to unlearn the way of ruin and misery
I think I'm broken under the rain

Epiphany Part 2: Failure

Failing – the motionless truth, like tiger's eyes tamed
that the innocuous heart burns in sight of distant towers
Beating with hourglass sand removed by tufts and flowers
and guitar rhythms rung, and the sheerness of stringent pain
For the sheer proclivity of understanding more than tongues and flames
Than revelation in the chaotic questions of the starry lamplit rain

Failing – and with grains of scriptured knowledge like stars
Scripted to understand more – whispered by groaning passengers
and grainy handfuls of sand spilled at coaches mark and stern
and grainy eyefuls of lamplight and starlight, left, right and barred
Standing alive before the eyes of the mourning streetcars;
Ask them. The blinding authors of ago, arrayed before the city's insane lure

Failure – outlining the dawn in window and eye-caught eruptions
And in turn, the epiphany annihilated doubt by a vision of lions
Like streams of sun breaking, good and strong
Through the hastened death of the stormclouds, with song
We are caught like those birds of calm, perhaps alive
forever, perhaps more, in the reach of many wayward roads
Will we gaze forever upon the healing and the harm?

Storm Authority

Storms fortify in flashes their own design
When atop the mountain lark and groans in hollow wonder
Wandered on breeze and wandered, stopping, uncouth, stood.
The mountain - The sired stonecutting folklore of raindrops
and maddening design calls the wind to power
and the wind returns to his feet, deceased.

The Forest

Singly does a leaf grow upon a tree
It marks the citizen in the midst of mystic night
And cloud patterns shed light like cobra skins
Upon parents of life in the hourless wasteland
Like pedestals to birds alone with the same performance
They and their fathers form the stormless throng
Scattering sun fortifies this powerful mortality
With stark truths against the sky of the passing word

Memory

Childhood and the deep dark ago.

"My conscience has a thousand several tongues, and every tongue brings in a several tale, and every tale condemns me for a villain. False face must hide what the false heart doth know!" - W. Shakespeare

Childhood

There is certain defeat in the silence
The silence of your diaphanous cloths
And in the poverty of boring torment
After endlessly puzzling voices
I sought the divine, fingers groping that dare not
Dare not touch the moon, nor any electric throne
Nor trembling voices address, nor ever say "answer me"

Silence. Speaking only of doorways
To hate, and evil, and prayer like a gladiator
hurling stars at the sun. The Bible opened,
And prayers flew like wind, in any weather, even torment
to that potent cutting wound at the wrist, a flame
Ears that heard hearts pain, reaching for
Bloodied voices, and words that dare not, dare not touch...

Once more the proverbial saying chimed: "I love you"
and she was sincere, it was deeper than Jacob's Well
artful, vindicated by sovereign honesty
They were calloused, though, by human loss
And grievous remains scattered on the floor
Laden with books on strange things: Aztecs, aliens and health
Somehow allied to the estrangement of family

It was a gunshot decision under ornate bright lights
One Ringed hand had opened, not quite Masonic, nor vampiric
Nor demonic. The disparate notion in childhood of alcohol
(Just remember how the Marie Celeste sank
or Nebuchadnezzar's fallen tree trunk stopped growing)
All savage reminders, piled high in the filth and the rubble
I finally, in all divine mercy, forgave.

Elegy of Timelessness

Watching!
They are watching!
They are in portents cast
by glimmers of grief
In reflections on the face of a dead TV set
The distinction of fire from smoke

It was not with excessive clarity
That I then understood
But rather with ironclad acceptance
Of the solidity of prayerful verse
Like the ineffable grace in a flower
A window opened into discovery

But my hands are made of fire
For I am not opposed to anything divine
I believe in light
In a kingship seen in ancestral memory
In a foremost prince in the sun
In fingers that allayed harm by his designs

This is my elegy
of living without time
And one day
It has to die.

Memorial

The sky and sea's abhorrent vast timekeepers call
Vocalizing whispers from beyond their walls
Echoing the word of death in the full daylight
As dust and mourning dissolves to white
Out of cupped hands, a lifetime flashes
The wind is full of their ashes
Leaving behind a quaking heart
That I bound and chained with sorrow's art

Siblings

The grief is illusory – the standards-
Are sacred family colonized
A vision of familiar love
inescapably held and memorized.
But the image; it's dissolving,
         melting
In a feeble mind taught unearthly diamond signs.

Love for me is how we sought timed, shared wonder
        in timeless hearts caught up
        in the promised song of forever.
But dreaming, always there, overhead and within,
Prophecy became minded under freedom bright skies.
In grassy heavenly valley, there I found her, one of them, again.
They were always there -like trapped starlight- like Tolkien's elven kin.
        I kept them safe behind that locked cellar door.
A foray, a sally, marching right through that door;
No more time to wrestle maddened dread;
I'd take deadened nerves and suicide instead.

"These are not healing tears":
I told Sarah in my dying heart,
in a distant vigil sealed.
As my fragmented eyes bled
This page here loosened one force to mend.
One more stand for a feverish endeavour
        grasping
            clutching
                eternal.
(I don't know how much more I can take)
In this, I know next to nothing;
"The best intent is when you sought for him,
        Not them."

Sisterly Potential

I released my heart
to the imagined sound of her weeping
And clouded by the crucial intent of believing
I sought a way to explain my dreaming

But sadness came in a sudden seizure
Knowing a distance far too great
Beyond causes in our control, love too late
The cause of her desperate nature, wildly innate

A prison, a prison, your smile belies it
No fault owned but what was chosen later
Little assurance now for a savior
An honest potential, built into a grief caricature

Like the clearing of a valley
Between mountainous ends
A name burns in unseen hand
My dream of you may forever last

I bear witness, to this skeleton of memory
The wild touch of misery killing melody
And bitter winds have passed me by
And bitter winds have passed me by

Sparrows - Short Version

When the storm clouds gather over the mountain
And the sea roars angrily from distant shores
Will you remember it is I who gaze with despair to where you are
And a journal of grief is written in desperation
As the sparrows flee silently into the bright midday sun

I saw
I saw lilies
I saw the sparrows
I saw the sparrows when I opened that Book
I saw the sparrows flee into the sun
This is what he said to me:
"Do not weep nor tremble"

I will write, weeping and trembling
In this journal of grief kept safely deep in my mind
About a place where we walked upon the horizon
The crystal shores went on forever
And the sun set upon an eternity together
I can no longer hear the roaring waves,
for I am miles away from the sea
I can't take my eyes away
Despite the ceaseless flow of tears
I just can't take my eyes away
From the sparrows fleeing
into the bright midday sun

Thoughts

We are an array of instrumental bell-hops
        (or automatons)
Reminders of your existence
        (or pain)
Open to change for a pocket full of change
        (we'll give you the keys)
Each one of us keeps his own room and door
        (and keyhole)
Comings, goings
        (sometimes less, sometimes more)
Flow of friends and enemies
        (channels and conscious states)

That room needs a locksmith
        (for good reason; this one has insomnia)
That one, a crowbar
        (logical effort)
And a certain measure of strength
        (practical wisdom)
Those are snakes! Don't go in there!
        (those are obsessions)
Here we cut off snake's heads
        (these ones bite, you have to kill them)
Sorry, that one's currently occupied by a special guest
        (ruminations)
If the fire alarm goes off, it's usually nothing to worry about, it's just loud
        (visual and/or auditory hallucinations)
The east hallway upstairs is off limits without permission
        (its not a secret, but Moses to John are kept there. In other words,
spiritual sacredness)

And behind the shed out back, you'll find Rene Descartes saying the same
thing over and over.

Pink elephants sometimes fly over the building. At times the hotel staff gather
to shoot them down with anti-aircraft artillery and rockets. A shortage of
weaponry is a problem, however.

In the basement you'll find some odd trinkets of deja vu, and forced canned
laughter.
        (anxiety, shellshock)

There is a mystical quality that we soberly dread in that last room, the one with the telescope aimed directly at the moon. On a full moon night. Perhaps its reverence for the Passover and the Lord's Evening Meal. Or maybe its the fear of werewolves. If you see a gigantic celestial show, remember not to enter this room. And never, ever look through that telescope.

(psychosis)

Saudade

Help me learn
Because for all I know
Sorrow lets love grow
Like roots drinking rain

And crazy sorrow can once more be sane
So answer to my agile grief
And we will carry each other's pain
on the wind-wracked skies forever

For a heart may sooner die
Before ever learning release
And this last cup of wine
Is for all who love that fades over time

Fault-lines

So often, once I woke, I would never dream a dreamless sleep
Nor swept away in halting shine, of their's, not mine
Belying the scattering mind,
Lies the torments of a clean shattering sign
So pervasive of their kind, of voiceless succour
Works grey success for righteousness, somewhere
In the senseless, sad compass point shouts
That bubble from the chest's inner star

The heart is an inner star
Complete in all it's division, arrows shot
At every foe and every devotion
United to the heavens' own halting sealed shine

It burns out catastrophically
Muttering senseless names on apostrophe lips
Apocalypse lips muttered to the lapse of family
of holy stars who are telling
                    (of violent secrets)
Massive grotesquery inside
                    (A division so utterly pervasive)
That less bubble minded inner works
                    (like burial mounds)
Cement the skeletal white blasting powder
                    (Covering his teeth)
And teach wisps of otherworldly sulphur
                    about clouded bleeding laughter in the lungs

(Go downstairs to burn the dark knots and fetters
No, no, no, snakes and stakes and a rod hold sway
But destruction is pensive, ashen, branded cold and hard
Drug dry blood turned ruinous)

Don't chain your heart, nor fault your sight
to the long, deep sleep of 'ago'
Nor prophecies, portents, and deja vu
And their singular unease within

Cascading through the wings of this wrecked mansion
Is the air of succour, this burning mansion
   (How many doors?)
Whips force one onward, a sojourn into the western mountains

The white law branded on his head
Within his mansion of a thousand doors
Never to tread near a dreamless sleep's burning
White lamps work for his inner star
   (Cremation sojourns in the light)
A positively elaborate mind, spirit or foe
   (Glued the sulphuric ashes to his lungs and teeth)
Dark knots lay the peace upon the sacred vessel
   (Harmful wavering laws of lawlessness)
With it's homeward details of bliss

   No long deep sleep.
   No downstairs.
   A journey
   All 'ago.'

Heart: Deathlessness

Wild in pain and doubt
I paused to collect myself
Flashed to a sight of an ash heap's elements
And trespassing homunculus hands hoarding ends

Caught on tufts in the breeze
I listened to aphorisms from a thousand
spirit addled trees. Carried leaf in hand within our time
Refuse trod by rainy foot, and intuited in aching spine

The heart I see is a curse and a captive warrior
I, glutted with feeble sleep and speech
See the heart is a thirst of agitated urge
Born new only in laws of foremost scribes words

The heart is a victim, and many victimless
A flask of unending parading nightmares
Author's coach or pen hand altered states
Beleaguered intuition, always with derisive fate

In veins of Vetruvius, that hand that writ
Miserable, crazed animal shouts of slavery
What do you know about the blood of madness
Leaking through my unraveling bandages?

This tankard in the centre
Of the meat about it, none of it a temple
A body of dirt, for collapsing house and rising grave
Destroy my heart's will to build, others to save

Meaning what?
Omnipotence and truthful harm, not martial
God's own humility sounds the horn
How could anyone deserve so much mercy, or is it scorn?

HEAT

A heated peril of the heart calls the sky
The sky whose hostly stare is starved and blind
And on the steps of heaven I wept
Over those like pure music that the flowers kept
Over them my faculty dwells
My groping memory and cherished hope

I am tired of bleeding from them
Tired of grieving over them
These tears are not a healing
And if I cannot mend
My heart will grow unseeing
And my mind, unbelieving

Torment/Restraint
-A Sapphic

The uselessness to learn little or nothing
How concomitant it is to stir dungeons
and cellars, robbing dust and breathing fire
Or seeing power

Smelling human mire, hearing faith, knowing
Works, tasting drink, feeling music and embrace
I shared these times with others, and on such a day
As this, bound to miserable libraries
I must confess false

My whole essential being has gone amiss
Whatever senses in me are lacking, I
saw a righteous bliss, I will appeal without
Enigma within

Longing recollection, with tranquility
Labors purity alongside clarity
As long as sister within memory lives
I, living, persist

And brother without truth exists, colliding
Coursed stars, is not relayed to hungry demons
little chips of broke erosion at my feet, all
reveals dust to dust

My savage shots of glance, gazing at nothing
All crannied flowers belonging to tired
Faith I will treasure, yet my heart adores song
in fuller measure.

Bindings

We want to live by each other's heavens
Not by each other's miseries.
So in this critical span
Bones must be set, inevitably we divide
And I fill my cavernous heart
With isolated meaning and terrible hope
Starving with flies and ash dispersing
but awake in beatitudes and sermons and proverbs
Let me heal frailty in what is not me
In what is not me nor you

Here's to love eroding over time
Here in mimicry, stage-fright, rocks and ruined hours
Heres to the end of the age in eternal ruin of towers
and all our love's conspirings, all its signs
and all it's binding powers.

OCD Heartful

I was a learned man once, learning
a way, taught to wander, not wonder
past the dull and graceless hurt
of hosted clouds, or break thru them,
like a shower, and trammels
of yesterdays coming, once more. I fought
a plague of eyeless obsessions again,
the psyche cyclops' bearing torment
in unbridled hands, yet again. pages flutter
in the ceased disturbance of my mind.

then knew I a power! and my eye
was hot with pain. my breath
a failing sign. and at last, heart
beating an unsound din:
Can I get up again
Can I get up again
Can I get up again
Can I lay down and ask for some burial
a mercifully evil kindness of dust
to cease all trembling for an end.

The Crescent Heron

Piers jut out among dwellings of communing fish
Under the shadow of white wings above the booming black lake
In treaty the jutting heart quakes with shadowed eyes

Tonight, once more taught through black dreams
and wandering pupils, never alone within
in the company of murky signs

They turn the fields of cancerous sleep in foamy furrows
In the slime and weeded marvels
I testify the calm with my sighs

And I'm stricken by how cold
the journey seems here, the belief
in leagues before a breath alights

I testify with each frozen toe
and fingertip that the calm
will never die

It is truer than the perils of the past
Truer than the worms and creeping evils
When something shuts the door below

And I echo with undoing the thunder in my heart
Without asking for more sincere trials
Thoughts ravaged by watery cries.

Our World Was

How frail the universe once can appear
A telling to construct again; being young
is in the iris: a constancy composing inner works.

Remember how the stars were too distant to comprehend
How skies are white with clouds of fear(and wish within higher)
How grass is taller than the sinking sun.

How the uncanny cricket channels the source of night,
How kings falter in old age, pride, murder and might,
And childhood memory is west of the living light.

There in the past- to everlasting gaze
As if the alchemist's impossible trick was won
Alight upon the globe of gold that our world was.

Aimless

An alchemical series: sun, sea, earth, wind. Based on thought from wandering and futility. The long turn of ages.

"Everything is futile!" - King Solomon, Ecclesiastes

Gott-natur, or the tone of nature:
It is not
- consciousness

- Sentience

- Psyche or intelligence

But: "grief; tears of things; slender sadness" (In Japan, mono no aware.)
Buddhists have associated this with the eternal wheel in reproduction;
Perhaps contemporaneous with the grave or Hades.

Aimless I: Sea

How treasured, how frightening
The dark ocean, full of gelatin lamps
Mystery temple for brave believers
Canvas for the privateer's blood
Worship keeps each foot grounded
Wracked knees shaking on the deck
Toes already writ in distant gleaming sand

For many months every hateful day was heavenly
By many prayers to fervent commanding sky
Fear burnt salt's sanctity on the whaler's tongue
Wind and fish mastery became the mast undone
Sirens and shipwrecks on glanced horizons
The end, the end, the end is not yet come
Captain, true captain to all these souls belong

But he by madness in anger and possessed fire
Passed arbitrary judgement on them without speaking
Dread sailor's conspiracy for the duly insane
Cadavers overboard and the smell of death in untended wounds
Fuming nostrils and groaning broken teeth beyond the test
No hope caught among this tormented throng
Celestial groping sounds the shining sea gongs
All watchtower and lighthouse vision beams must be wrong

Impelled by commanding hunger
To the blessed earth they remember
Never seal the eyes with sleep
To priest, believer, and seafarer's pace
A singer climbs on the waves
Calling, shouting at lungs top bellow
Hopeful storm of words and names

Once more into the battle
Once more into the fray
Once more into the waves
keep honor and trust and fuel for the brain
Sweet fruits and longlasting life will tell
This is no apparition
But the calamitous drum of our ark's death knell

Aimless II: Heaven

As if suddenly heavy with child
The great clouds birth happy birds
Sparrow, thrush, chickadee, beloved
Presence of soul within the glory span
There's a spirit in the wind

They soar down to the rock
Feathers clad in waterdrops
Tending with simple beaks
The balance of soil between
Clutter, weeds, and prized seeds

The hermit's vision is here among them
For the seed of man dwells before.
And watching above the heavy horrid rise
Of crag, oath and doom
Comes the clownish, clashing
Laughter of the unclean
Vile ones, ravens.
To him, they are first of criminals
Allies to the snake
Eyes like twin lamps lured
To the length of his shame
His memory of a studied age.

With watchful trek
and longing for days of chess
He climbs the last cliff,
guarded by the coming storms.
His threadbare life longs to gaze into eternal night
That trail the planet's plummet into black depths
His wrinkled salutory face seeks future again
Expressed now in rags, a noble might jarred and thin.
Man brought low by unguided epiphany,
wisdom, and sin. It seems to him
that the pure sky smiles back
through the sad wind.

The owl will wait
Upon his throne of hemlock branch
For one wiser than him.
And the moon will chase
all mysterious dreams
under the waves
As the world's voices grow dim.

Aimless III: Earth

The earth sold it's bloom, its blood, its company
Of man - to the dreadful dynamic deceits
In sky, grave, and gasping land
Look ahead!
Yet have faith in the approaching mountains
I believed in one's unearthly might
A faith in great cliff's towering counsel
To walls of wisdom arrayed with powers
Set before all as godly sight

The star sold it's admirer, its progeny, its witness
Of Man - to the fearful forsaken night
With it's black lakes, morgues and dreaming snakes
Look again!
Yet have faith in the rock
Climb to reach the pinnacle where eyes lock
To where you've been once before
Grieving from insanity through the wounding hours
Long apart from love and life of scouring sisterly flowers

The perfect law can breathe its judgement
Against this half-bodied catastrophe
The wild tongue sentences to death
My own ways belong to curses
I am not above such a garbled test
I cannot sleep but beg for rest
I cannot sleep but beg for death.

Aimless IV: Sun

The sanguine unsung heavenly power of descent
Coddled the pangs of rising fear that trembled
The songbird hearts of unsacred children
Raised by a generation of wordless drunks
Who without having them taught, nor the Teacher
Confirmed the cunning happiness, stirred a coming sea
All in their own errant lack and loss, under the clouds
Without innocence, lamb nor dove, told in the signal
Let not their eyes now forget the things they have seen under the sun.

He now that cherishes the child and bird and beast
May once know the beginning of this mercy, upon
Reaching the restless place of grave and shining sign
and unmarked land at once, complement to that sign
With a worn out handful of sand, and a human dilemma
and a terror blooming over the sea, shadows within a conquest
Then learns that perfect teachers are those born by all of perfect hope
Some sworn to secrecy and sealed by the stake and hangman's rope
Let not your eyes now forget the things you have seen under the sun.

Songs of Hope

Hope and travailings.

"Sometimes I go about pitying myself, and all the time I am being carried on great winds across the sky." - Ojibway saying

In the Place of Mourning

There was a human angel who told me I had a name
I gave her everything I had for the chance to be sane
Certain woman of olives, fragrant pearls of pleasure
Oil of her body was in a perfect ephah measure

"Hold onto me as lilacs bloom
Promise me you'll embrace the soft playfulness of the moon
We are still as he is, ancient children, innocent too soon
Among fertile fireflies doting over lapping pools.
See how his full face is marked,
Like the delicate clarity of etchings on a coin
Composed of atomic truth
Mark the solemnity on the back, Whatever face
Regardless of identity
is like the face of a faithful young boy."
The full flames of heaven meddle with the past, with innocent toys
You told me in childhood
How the ocean is more beautiful in the dark
Perhaps its the passivity or the grace
The ash heaps are speaking, shouting about ruinous release
About the forsaking of pillars of fire in a greater past
Now is the time for courage to last
For the horizon is giving birth to final storm clouds.

Katie

Surrounded by the sun
We are the trio shadow of one
Here in the crudity of daylight
The systems of trivial,
delicate evils
Every day was stolen from me
For what its' worth
I counted the stars with you
In my head and heart forever

For all that I know
Sorrow lets love grow
What did you say to me
"Don't leave me"
Dont you understand this means forever
It meant to me vaster than an ocean
And one step in the wrong direction
leads to sane

I can't endure it
No one can save her
No one can save
No one can save her
I can't endure it
Death before death
My spirit's bearing down
Your light rests in my hand
I can never feel again

For all that I know
Sorrow lets love grow
Let go of the ocean
Dreams rest in my hand
The world grows around you in my eyes
Place your thought near me
Never fail the feather's burning
I will chase you like a bird closer to the sun
You promised me not to slip away forever

Dreams rest in our hand
You are near me again
whispered love, a life song
Even on the surface it burns
I cant endure that pain anymore
No more
No more
No more.

Mercy's Parameters: a sparrow's thoughts on a near death experience

my cat caught a bird. He brought it home to me still alive. I let it go. These are his thoughts

Today is wrong skies; orange thunder, pillows to look at
Level headed mercy from them, or mosaics
here to now. Home to lovejoy
A pattern ago
the lodestar failed
I was following the boat
to human's doom
Blind Yes!
Ignorant No!
Fresh out of faith
Freshly shipwrecked
Stale mate lives, seeds and signs
each digit on the leaf marks
heart crystalline tree time, many of them
Forestry radiant errors, they are crowned
below me, colloidal color and flames
Plummet underneath me
I want to live free

Live. Vitality. Live
Guidance. Stars
Sky. Stay
Stop.

Going on in blind faith
Chords and clouds mingle, better seeds unsown
But
There is a prowler near
The catcher!
Overwhelm, power struck! ripping
violent lightning
I have never
before seen
it is not
orange nor
chirping
it is my pain and my
hurting fear song break

cry out
cry
cry
cry

into the protection vocality
Chanting comfort zone
Listen. Breathe. Stop.
Yes. No. Yes.
human to bird binary
When in the labyrinth teeth caused hurt
The bells stopped
but the sound is still coalescing, clicking
by sundry, radiant flowers outside. Crowns of, wreaths of-
A broken wing,
"You can still hop"
The throes of annihilation stop.

Live again. Vitality. Live again
Guidance. Stars
Sky. Stay
Last.

Resonance

A voice cut through
A dream, unsafe
Resonating in my head
"We'll read your peculiar mind" it said
"Starved of endings that endings defined
There should have been
A sword in your hand
An option of escape
Written in suicidal stars
Restless at daybreak
Did you know differently?
Did you read volumes of iniquity?
Did you know how?
To aspire to the killing sky
To feel the aspect of breathing
Under a westering sun
Pretend once again, to be
Represented, be remembered
your brother, your sister, every time
You look in the mirror
unending shattering rains."
Then came the end

Awake.

Watcher's Love

I set my feet upon a crag
Heart formulas equate a valley between us
Sparrows took flight
Towards an open door
Enamoured and dressed in delight
I will bathe in your liquid sight

Time has come to prove to us
What you really are
Your own path
I dreamed that you will reach
Your own goal

We are a shooting star
We can't be wrong
Maiden you will rise
And you will fall
If you want you can stand upon a crag

Reach for the sky and then you will make it
Realize that you really are
Sun will say you will fade
Expressions closed away from us
Where is the light that shines
brighter than lanterns

In grim days you chose to remember
Who you really are
Mountains are true to you
Inciting chants, violin keepsakes
War shouts pledged to your cause

Wavering, everchanging in lifetimes
Time has come to prove to us
You will know you made it
Prove to me that you really are
You will rise
and you will fall

If you are brave you can handle all
Reach for the sky
Handle all fire
Realize that you really are
Lanterns closed your eyes
awakened bright like calls shattered

From bedside you will be remembered
For who you are
Time has come to prove to us, people are seeing
Choose your own path
Reap and you will reach your cold design

Like scattered light you are a shooting star
You will make it
You will rise
you will fall
If you really are
You can stand tall for all time

If you really are awake
Sun will say
You will fade
Vengeance closed
Your answers threw away your witness

You are everchanging, bright like a lantern
In God's grace you rose like a star
Proven by weather and storms
A proven witness
That you really are
You will make it.

Eternal – the Mountain(Sapphic)

See the failing whirl of the leaves of despair
Fly with the anchorless miseries of man
Their one motion has turned to his wisdom
Sights of the holy.

His flaked, chaff skin smolders, scatters, seeding ash
Across the gold grasses, silent fears within
their wake. A bygone day, now an author's hour
with trembling hand.

Her inexistent fingers damascened, clutched
And sung to him from the weaves of oldest sands.
Flights that fared over what seemed inescapable
demands love forgot.

Nothing and symbols of nothingness hold sway,
All submission in meaningless tears' burning.
This is the peril of writing with nothing:
Horizons eternal.

Perils of tirelessness without guidance,
Nor remembrance constant hue, a bygone hour
Was fatal, in tall grasses concealed the truth
their gold faulted sway.

Starlit, starlight, black agencies and distance;
The catharsis of thousands in the garden
Of earthly delights. Blood with mercy, amid
This conflagration.

A nightmare or memory, when the red dread
and somber furnaces burning darkly bright
Glow in drains and vents and gasping hellish light,
Evil eyes turned and wept.

And there is a potential shift of insight,
Family in the fragrance of loss and drift,
And under the sink, in sewage death grieves many;
No deliverance.

There's more fear and error and captivity
In this powerless witness terror, than doomed
implications under raging moons' command;
A horned call to fight.

Their warnings contained in a mad sorrowing
Corners of strong rocks lend a hand, his eye sees
and seals and locks, as memory boils, he knows;
Pain no more the call.

The choirbound music in this climbing love
of galvanized voices, at once on mounts above
sounds the musical clink of shell, coin and ink;
Endlessly bounding.

Once like a denarius in the fish mouth
once for him, one for her and whoever hears
The song, bending war for a world without wrong
this great ancient song.

Katie, Sarah, 2

White sands turn soft
Fill your palms with refracted light
The glory of the Grecian sun
In romance and all final wars
Like understanding Revelation-
Save yourself from breath and decay
Like an hour of salvation in the sun
Wash the blood of me in the sea
I will find you again – on the horizon I held for you
Safe from temptations all in the beyond
All vanities-flowers, and anthologies of them
The poet's once lost on me – and I found
Found in grey to white – your pulse
And many who are last
will be first
Jehovah writes on the heart
I will write your's in the implacable waters
with unacquainted severe fingers of life
Until the sea churns over
and all it's sands bake in the sun
My heart, your heart – one vanquished, one never won

It was dying
I'll believe in nothing again
Just so I can hold onto you
to your singing cells – the everlasting
I believed for you to sing, what my heart brings
The lost in future, even then,
would be too much – too violent
Too far sorrowing – still I watched you recede
Time unbelieving, my own vigilance failed
Like the mountains crumbling into the sea
All visions become the past long gone

Then it left me in a place
Without you. A break, a validity, a state,
desperate like dying flames, coming cold,
shining temptations, speaking of callous fate
And an end

                an end
                    an end
                        an end
It's not too late.
I have to believe in you, in myself
For our sufferings here - golden and grey
have sundered the hearts of too many before
it's not too late.

The Living

In feebleness, born in weakness
walk in mystery, catch the foot in error
And each night, eat your fill of slumber
Where the swirling pond is dripping
Where deserted hopes are cold agates slipping
Where long before great storms conspired
above the waterless awake earth
Become whole and one in secret with them
Guarded and watched and silver dim
The horn blows, cascading metals
Wake up!

Where the Birds Fly

In the house infested by snakes, gathered
In the upper rooms, there are finishing voices,
lingering in echelons of language,
with a deafening mythological madness
subduing the truth without secrecy
"Why? Why? Why?"
I heard her keep saying, with secret tears
and confusion unformed.

Imagined or communicated,
A nightmare later or before
It was spoken with so much pain
and screaming grief, I imagined
myself burning. A loved one,
telling a fragment, the birth of dread,
martyrs and life in filthy goblets
Life fatal message, my seashell token

Winded and struck with horror
Who am I, that I wrestle with the maddening,
Unable to shut my eyes! How else can I see beyond,
the necessity of beyond? Past discordant cries of anguish,
ahead of sinister and suspect spiritualisms?
They being an elusive bauble in the garbage can
of my heart. Blind and sick with horror
I said with suffering: No. No. No.

But there are secrets in the seashells
and in frustrated plans of wing
and frustration in loose feather scattering
There are ones, staring, burning
with the sun. Boring holes in the sunny clouds
With their eyes of unsettling pain
"Where the birds fly" a child may utter innocently
much like the secrets in the seashells

And vanquished and unchanging, with cries
of anguish, the birds of heaven fall ever upwards,
ever great, ever severe, over the conspired,
unwatched crimes. This round polished
seashell, new secret alive in the heart,
Whispers with the children of paradise, saying:
"Where the birds fly"
Where the birds fly.

Hope
the sparrowsong

"Is it not hopeless?" they sing, certain
to guard that which sings, that which
says: "I will guide you home."
Free to fulfill in the why and now, flames that endure
So feebly do I hope. Caressing scorched eyes
One bone sawn apart to form one belief
No more – exhaust from rib skinny trees
No more – pallor of a thunderhead rising
No more – bloodied groans held down and coffin bound

It is the last sorrow song of a deliverance
Now abstracting the glow of fate
Inhabiting but one desire:
to care less, to live and know certainty great
To guard the talking sparrows in their song
Over a low broken wall by the road, Guard
the very last and only one, next to the corpses
The remainder in his heart that sings:
"Is it not hopeless?"

Zero-Point Strife

There's what seems
a neverending scene ahead
covers over my eyes once more
I have other hands to reach for help
But a collapsing horizon failed
Scattered the coals of the sun
And we both know, my teacher
every day is once more a rage, a race
Nobody returns unchanged
from this war a warrior
Neglected by man
the finish line
never a blind reproach
My peace so near
Nobody returns

Kingdom Girl

Kingdom Girl.
A romantic paradigm.

Kingdom Girl I

My eyes and face tingle with gladness
with delicate admiration over her form
There is a womanly power about her
Her bosom, gladly clad in dark spark-dotted dress
Where sensuous gloom meets
with daylight fire
like stars receding
into ornamental finery of the sun's garment
The light in her face takes precedence

Gaze straight into her eyes
where the sun is,
eyes teary with cosmic dust
It is gazing also into midheaven
where birds call
her lascivious hair flows
a flower amidst flames
the compassion within her
an anointing in a pool of serenity

Kingdom Girl 2 – The Singer

I refuse to concur- nor consumed by bitter lure
Or cravings of flesh whose sin churns
But her crown lies in her candle eyes
In lady's oval joy of proud fresh cheeks
And signed above her diademed brows
I see how her fury attends to grace.
This intricate invitation in her hair,
but in her voice overwhelming
as a ringing prayer.

All collude to full-bodied desire
A cascading song of lips
As musical as lyres
Her intent then
I could not fully percieve
That watchers produced her gift
Is true. She, a holy singer,
like a white young angel
To my childhood calling
an omen of calling,
calling
Calling
past the dark.

This power is burning

Feminine guile and womanly art
The power to subdue
the wrath of man,
by gold glory
forming
heart
New.

Kingdom Girl 3

(Form: Pindaric Ode)

Her feet are mixed in corpses of leaves
Mired leaves and water unstagnant stirred
They touch together, brown of skin and leaf
the occult hue of a chapel door opened
Envied painted toenails, and she drinks from glass
With a curtained steel glimmer in her eyes
A spun cup, bottomed with pearls, portents cast
from her lodestar gaze in a mirthful guise
Shining to rise higher, to find her home
Lure in her fierce flowing gaze disclosed

Would I find the reign of my fear of her
The conflicted sight shows this in marked signs
Where dominant is my leaf heart flutter
That her intricate vivid form entwines
Perhaps there is a sweet peace in her pearls
Or the name for the color of desire
Radiating like spiritual flame curls
In tracings of heavens maps conspire
To guide by the civil stars' written code
Whose laws in her fine fabric garments sewn

I do not know even her name nor origin
For she spoke it with a mystery
There must be a wealth of youth and growth and gesture
there in her glowing body of gold
What am I but a vessel of burned out need?
That same true white anchored candor in her feet
Toes together, leaves fell from the trees of sin
Both touch a full and delicate thought
Of all she contains and mires within
I will touch her lodestar
With the edge of a knife
Meditate on the absence of wind
Finding her for the very first time again

Kingdom Girl IV

Let these things not be hostile
I want living, bold and sure hands to seek for help
Let the perils under sun weaken and peace' endurance destroy them
Here in the seat of the fire
Outside, she was a deliverance of symbiotic,
flower-rayed cellular wonder
Inside, a catastrophic collapsing horizon
failed.

Her hand, treated by delicate fingers,
outwardly spoke of febrile command-
Less touched to my dramatic decay of hope
and in it's stead vibrance of youth and great
godly virtue of an unadorned form
Not a ring, not a mark. My belief crawled
past her wrist, up her arm and rested
on the robustness of her breasts
And in sight of star to kindling star
of eye pupil to eye pupil,
crowned and rayed with delicious black
Undamascened fingers to full bodied scorn
I was captured, like a bird, and was overcome

What is beauty but one singular gleam in the eyes
that speak to the sparks of all
marvels and moments, born in heavenly violence?
A life forced trapped light in a photographic
prison of a distant, distinct time and call?

And all words are
captured and bound, whether beautiful
or bland, bold or musical.
All are bound to fail.
Save her name, gracing alien lips
Taught like a child to succumb
to her, only her true luster.
Her vivid motion between tress
and livid toes, truly
How incomplete I feel without her,
One to belong to me reciprocally
in a nugget or facet of momentous sky's time.

114

How incomplete, how
Incongruously desirous of only her finery,
even of just one strand of her
preciously shining hair
or one aromatic fold of her fine garments
I will make flower arrangements that
do not decay for her
Bouquets whose only alternative to breathe
is to scorn the spiraling pit
What vista of ocean warmly touching clouds
Knows anything about the symmetrical treasure
of gazing upon her furnace hot gold face?
Hearing the tinkled bells of her
murmurs and living laughter
She is a soul I cannot hope to fulfill
to her own granted justice
What justice demands of riches beyond
all prior gates of pearly-clad meaning
I have her truth only in my heart and mind
I cannot justly ever claim such one

Bathe then will I in her crystal liquid grace
sightful starlight will tell her
how I loved her for the briefest spans
and the most audacious terms
in tents camped before eternity

Kingdom Girl V

I became lost, charmed in a vision
First I saw her black hair turn, toned, and shine
Halfway down her sibilant body
Then gleaming with the great white willpower
of the red and haughtier sun.
It was the truly full teeth of cats
Or words read in the pages of a wise book
With dust and castle sands, all below her feet
All burnt before the pitilessness, the pestilence
of her red filigreed dress and sable crown

"There is such a severity of beauty to her face"
I mumbled placatingly within.
"Like punk rock or metal. Like guns.
Too severe to be wholesome
Too much the air of the authority in the world
Yet, she must be significant. This air must be infinite.
Due to a 'biker babe' mentality ensuing before her
A man's heart crushing, in throes
A severity that is too much,
too much to be pure.
She is another full enigma."

Would it take one more omen, one more capture
to understand the cage of mortal, guile beauty
or the dials of a compass mind?

She's just a girl, after all.

Kingdom Girl 6(VI): A Cage

For years, I sent out a pale white love bird
for her, patterned with so much undoing
Staggered with undone devilry,
A silence in her hair, and unforgiven ways
How insight and yearning by high
                    Powers
they shake they
                    Abound.
For the must haves of steadier Hearts.

I being witless, down into her blaze
a forest filling brown, a labyrinth, maybe chapel
of destruction and devotion, and I percieving
two and plus great lambent eyes
Have felt her gazelle-horn gaze
wildly sung as an overwhelming stave
In the dictation of a forest emptied
Over dark grasses and a crescent forever
A forest now empty empty empty, how how
Many many bereaved fringes Remain.

Is it petals? Is it snow?
Her breasts full like blossoms.
Turn the stars in your burning hair, I said:
And she rose, lying, decieving, with a clasped bracelet
for calling rituals more of what more is Dead.

Romantic Poems from all author's timespans

Romantic poems from all author's time
spans(excluding Kingdom Girl)

The paradigm of red.

The Moabitess

Around the earthly midnight hour's measure
I spoke to a dismal star
Whose deathly gloam I treasure
"What if your constant light
Is really another world like ours
For your spark sang to my good pleasure
It is a pragmatic art
To place such heirarchical terraces
Within our sight."

For on the same night
Shimmering strands of watery moonlight
Are cascading, terraced, down the palace waterfall
Of her ebony hair
If that dismal star is true
She sang apart to my believing heart
With all the clamor of that distant world
From tressed crown to enameled feet
Her braided glory, her magnetic force
See what power her beauty commands!
In her eyes like starlight tokened to my heart
To longlasting delight

Together, we won't be left to chance
Nor coupled with the unforeseen
For at the core of divination
In the heart of oracles, by gazing distant star
Your priestess gown is glowing, white hot
With damascened quartz and copper bangles
In silence I act to temple's candles snuffed
I can hear your gentle footfall
from constant star to us
Peace of three
and soft pieces of wax now burn,
now melt on the floor
Like my beleaguered heart

Nadia

Nadia, who is a flower of stalled beauty, allows
me to sleep, sit, and reminisce
Under dark colors of her contemptual clouds.
She wanders along trails of blue leftover diamonds, fully enriched.

Sparks dance along her glowing legs, thighs and baroquian top.
Her eyes of burnt egg amber, breasts of crayon vibrancy and elegant
topless forms posing threat like a bird trap
She possesses a serene, sunblessed glory of spirit's want.

Her quizzically blank expression is possessive of a sleeping one,
For she sleeps as she walks with downcast powdered eye-lashes.
Her hoops promote a visceral vision, like the sun
(How very black her bright blonde hair flashes.)

A form that bright, that unusually shining,
Emits the glow of a pharaonic, golden countenance,
visceral and severe. in her I feel an imprisoning,
promising decadence, thriving debauchery; along the Nile she hunts.

Her auric fields of vision silence me, various thoughtless
Traps by straps lifting breasts, lifting cruelty and dismay
Of Babylon's towers, Of no flow to the lust
Thinking of her is a clear treatment of ecstasy

I imagine there are rooms full of her screams, bliss, perfume scent,
and insolent love, seductions without a heart.
The glory of her hair is an intricate invitation of intent,
To percieve her will is eternal made short.

So I admired her without words
"How very fluid your fingertips of ruby viscosity."
"Be mine!" she whispered in answer, in sexual fervor,
A fairy's floating hiss high up in the windy stones of enmity

I answered "Stay alone" adding to a sound
of waters sullied, stopped up
In the dark places of a well, and high above ground
Ecstatic cries of raven's, by various tricks resound

Thus dreaming I ask her, as her beautiful, blue scaly timed eyelids bloom
Onto a field of cathedral disparity
"Where is the room to sit with only you?"
Amid the Nazi paintings by stereo and graffiti

Now outside the door, a dread and greatness as of water rushing
An ebbing tide along the coast of body, her riches
"Female, Femail, FEMAIL" her messages against the door are crashing
Her feet, her brilliant tight toes painted with serpentine liquids

Her voice is lilting, lyrical, absolutely musical, carrying feminine hue of her
wish
Reach those livid, outpouring lips, and her hips are eagles cherished
To a fault, a flaw, a formula, without a scream
My most desperate vigil, lying on a bed of mice, unseen

Remember only her mystically wanton face
born of apples and sips of Capricorn tea, in each drop
There are locusts fluttering in her lamp of silky terrors, full of grace
Peacefully pondering sleep in auras of rapture, peace, and solace

Blonde bombshells like Nadia
cause no manly grace, only desks
full of tape and refuse, paraphernalia
"How to tie a tie" and other tests
great moments in her historic driven escalade
Fruits and other sweet miseries were in her eyes
Her sepia-ensconced eyelashes amaze
The longing pours out, no end to stuttering stop signs
Her cheeks, likened to pears, of shimmering flowery almonds engraved
and apples, perfectly aligned, full of praise

No end
Alike in symphony
She dazzled me
By brilliant quartz degrees
under royalty and decrees
of her faint embodied boldness
Nowhere to go but up, upwards
A call of insight
She fondly admonishes
"Try not too much"
No end to the sight of her

Red

Her name was not Jessica Rabbit
Nor Hayley Williams, for that matter
But cutting her red tresses
Would be like clipping an eagle's feathers
An endangered species on top of that
She is a terraced waterfall of blood
From crown to waist, a dream is in her hair
A fiery succubus playing glorious red ocarina notes

So at the knifepoint of unbroken hermitude
Secluded to summon her blazing image
With dormant eye fixed on her perpetual fall foliage
Obsequious toward the facets
The facts of fascinating radiance
I asked a burning question:
"Can one woman's smile
Heal a man's heart?"

"Like knitting a garment together"
Her burning laughter said
I knew then as my heart dripped
like red candle wax to the floor
Cool peace would overtake me
(Though she is an enigma full of explosions)
Because of unutterably melodious hues of red
In the rhythm of my bloody red heart

Solomon's Daughter

Without ever looking to heaven or sky
Over sacred span of lustful sighs
The sable beauty's gaze is to household treasure
Solomon's black 'daughter of Jerusalem'
Focused in her attractions

There is the shine of eyelashes in her pride perfected airs
Licentious larceny in scattershot glances
Verdant in feminine nature
Or heart bedecked dress, so much longing
Her fruitfully glossed breasts are the curse of too much bonding

Bondage of sparkling eyes, luscious lips
and lashing moans in immodest dress
Emanations like the hum of an engine
The halo round her head is the center of heaven
Her thoughts were towards Inanna as she gazed up

It takes a polymath to understand
the depth of her intricacies
Her voice is high-pitched, lyrical
Rapid in strange places, absolutely musical
She gives her song for free

There is a treacherous clarity in her sky
Like moving through motions assigned
By forces around us, unknown
It is as if she is
Commanding the stars to break forth
To shine in jubilant declarations
Co-conspirators in sight of reverie
She gave her song to me

Lady, Absent

Woke up to an unsolvable crime
My worst fear is bearing down
The lights are too bright
I dreamed a dreamy breeze caressed her hair
The world goes all around four walls
Without her
The light is burning
Body of flesh covered by tapestry
in burst of modern red dress
The thrust of lovely breast, emanations
Within her
Her light is too bright
Spirit slain by the enticement
In scattered love, absentia
The seeds of change, change life
Together with her
The light is so bright
Nor will great wise red sun rise
Without marking the birth of the rest of the sky
She was the light I longed for

She Was Not Waiting

Sparks work their secrets about the stationed waterfall,
Ring contained blasts in the proclamation of holy smoke.
The visitor's destiny to breathe the mist from lungs to crown to star.
Taught thereof in celestial vein of the rainbow's righteous coil.

Virtuous dead branch near on the rocks plead the deserving hope
So speaks the midday union of green youthful yearning:
"Let us again gain power in sunlit mercy
Above perilous freedom for the godly deserving."

He lifts the branch, the bud on it is dying
The life falters in his comfortless eyes. A prophecy:
She was not waiting, nor was she spurning
Sudden end, like a flashing knife to the peacefully enduring.

An hour more travails on heart's leftover destruction.
The last moment was known like dogma: loss of a promise
And whispers burn in edge of hearing promising familial strife
Falling march of waterdrops timed to murmurs of unsettled pain.

Defiance

You are a soft voice in my brain
Supple, soft, that says: I am soft,
Supple, red like apples tumbling ,
from a queeny throne. Tumbling,
royalty of curse word camaraderie.

Hoops and Hopes

Her hoops gloated her face between sun-red ears,
silhouetted in holy diamond bearing remarkable.
They watched the seagulls turn their terror inward
In their fighting flight to the sun, to be
the never returning, the horizon call,
For those on shorelines reclining in heaven's absentia.

And the gloves of my sister's gift
turns away the frost,
covers inerrant loves, the absence
singing, a rope on Niagara like a cloth of blue.
Fingerprints of scrying, the red out the window
for this: an electrum vision, the falling walls

Therefore, I will read into the storm by you,
Heart wild with trespass and fear.
Like a touch of lightning with vict'ry,
Certain eyes of stoicism to it's falling,
crashing west, my crippled hands, this is how
you put out the fires.

A theocratic judgement does not err.
Perhaps to cut off the right hand it must be.
But this is madness!
And in sight of the flawless,
there is revival, in vivo, before the calamity
of unpaved roads.

Two sparrows, two gulls, the sun
And more than anything, the Word.

Sebastian and Whimsy

Poems of my cat, and other whimsy(such as elves.)

Sebastian

Verily, my cat has fattened paws,
and pride in gallant ears
and protests me with clucklemouse squeaks
Verily, My cat is plump
his glinting serpent eyes
are either divine or demonic
Depending on who notices
Verily, he is a reflecter of evil
Guardian of tombs and granaries
champion of the birdcatchers
but unlike the devil
He throbs his heart to fill my lap
Verily, padding plop in summer rain
he is immune to disgrace
My shouting is met with plaintive cries
Verily, he is certain of my unreasonableness
Expecting his dinner at half past 5
But I know I'm never his master
Verily, he returns from the night only out of pity
Knowing Ill perish from hunger
he deposits the kill to keep me alive
verily, by grace, to find mice, to show me with simple trace
and he keeps us both warm, he thinks
fighting off the demons at night without batting an eye
Verily, still, he must keep his claws sharp
So I box his ears to his pleasant delight
Verily, verily, truly I say unto you
He and I are the best of friends

Sebastian II

There is both fiefdom and doldrum flames
In my cat's pupils.
Enshrined in avoidance against
human oddities.
Pride, patience, and boredom
Only arisen when seeking
night dweller prey
He thinks there are inscrutable lessons
In the hands of Master
Saying: "I've both learned more and seen more
Than for hosts of reasons to ascend upright
I will remain on four and lickshine my fur
ensorcelled by my purrs."

The Bear that Speaks

The bear is the wisdom of boring beasts
A brown, necessary, and druidic mass
Garbled monster born of horn drunk dreams
That brought honey-sweet veracity for diviner's means
and stand-in as a killer for mocked prophets

His broken claws are the source of the forest's austerity
Plodding trustful paw keeps the black soil firm, the earth round
Each awful giant step shutter stops the sun-to-earth clock
Yearly withdraws into a wintry ignoble death
The bear is the stalwart, the bastion against disease

Integrity

Whack! Went the walking stick-
"Old age – it requires
a self-addressed envelope
Blurred, containing dead photographs
No return stamp, no glorious crown
Over grey wheezing hair
By the pillars of Atlas' arms! By me!
One potent glazed gaze
A step up to every insolent kid
Looking down in naive pity
Christ the King is white haired too!"

Tinfoil

Even in the darkest times
we wore flimsy hats
baseball, fedora-
breeding throbbing skulls within
their tall power of cocooning, blooming...-
...-'Thoughts?' I'd asked the man with swastika eyes
and of gazing telepathic misery
who doesn't see me, either initially
or intentionally. My pupils
must be swirling, because I remember
India in the Punjabi face I saw last week
(his Christian candor hangs over the loss of a brother)
'Hello?' I ask again, with long
far away ocean tidal crustacean throat humming
'Speak!' Replies the telecommuner in
the ocean watching place
I question only – then with my heart
on the battlefield, with a great outcry
the great outcry of temple knight and modern soldier
of Christ: "Lead us!'
so I question only – then with my mind
make sure my black cap fully covers my brain before listening
'do computers and cellphones circumvent God's designs?'

I remember – Terence in a fedora
and trenchcoat, his starlet the voice of Annie Lennox
his Masonic affirmations as he mocks the idea
of angels. So I ask him about them
his neck is red, like raw meat of a shank of beef
"Do they have wings?" he replies with mockery
driving the point home by mimicking flying saucers

I recall that his theories about angels were decidedly morose
the governance of computers over all Creation
Jesus and God nowhere in sight, except as a guffaw
in a backyard play of Straight Flush among old man poker games
or a home run in the baseball field of human error
and the existence of only good and bad aliens

I remember how the Bible said the same thing
(in the latter case) with different diction and substance
and crisscrossing Gehenna and a sure to fall city, five years later
I recall how we first met, along Egypt's banks, pyramids
and dung beetles guided by cosmic interference

I hope he is resting, content, with less of an open mind
and a fedora that can bring the sunlight,
double sunlight solace of true unaddled sanity
beyond the closed walls like a circus fortress for
all and any composed spiritual and literal drunks
much like him, and me, before I smashed every bottle
and gripped my head in the vise of the eternal Book

One day someone might ask me what went wrong
I hope I will only have to answer them what went right

Elven Spirituality

They spoke for the values of beauty
Vivid monuments to an everlasting force

They being merciful dreamers of unity
In starry laws heed the inspired voice

Traces of healing comforts, their priest's poetic refrains
Severe quick life fingers, a touch halts decay

Their wise designed temple reliefs with water and signs
Telling wanderers who fear the echo of horrible wars

About the crash of their falling cities
And about tales of a first end long before

About the poverty of beautiful pondering
And the white galleries of quiet trivial arts

About the bells of twilight years tolling, telling
To forget any remnant glimmers of hope

They spoke for the values of beauty
Like the echoes between the stars

Stern thought beyond the tragedy, with kingly austerity
Beyond the snares of the enemy; cruelty and coals.

Maidens young sprinkled tears on their sons
The sealed symbol's of ancient warrior's forms

One soul of their's was an unbending fire, a binding valor
Drunk on the deathless music and named for his arm

For such was there jealousy above the adversary's gates
The long gaze of the wicked, fuelled by constant hate

No longer do they sing, no longer do any believe
Stripped of all forms with science and unease

Persevering age is spent, but their memory stands guard
In ruins ageless as the sun; mortal man cannot hold the flame.

Darkness

Relegations of pain, grieving, devastation, and the long human constancy of suffering.

"If there is a match, don't leave even a match behind."
- D. Pollitt

Authority of Darkness

Where faithful angels overawe men
              so that hopes in heaven die
Where filth of graffiti and calls of unclean birds
              contend for demonstration of arrogant signs
Where realization leads to pallor clad skin,
              grey fear and heightened blood
Where following the terror of beings of aberrance
              calls to deep places in a mind that succumbed
Where fowls regurgitate in maddened states
              under a bleating sky gone mad towards midnight tests
Where salamanders tread and serpents crawl
              dwelling in the orifices of morgues, sightless
Where critically destructive trapezoids abound above
              and by their presence bring men to their knees
Where fluttering pennants atop towers in a civilian wind
              are strong inspiration for violence in the roaring seas
Where sorrowful potentates rule over pits
              Forming the hour of pain
              I, for one, was too blind to ever pass by
              Potential granted and given: understanding, wisdom and time
Where these things exist
That is where the authority of darkness lies

Big Pharma

On the view of brilliant world's glory,
sunrays shotdown an armada: ships of fools
All wisdom's children stumble from cemetery to cemetery
searching for a stroke of fire, a rifle shot, a spark or flash
of contemporary inspiration, the yield of a lash
To finally relax, an end to the scourge

But there is no precious light here
Only primeval conditions, the constancy of bitter daylight
Seen first on the shoulders of giants
Freud and Jung and Foucault
Restructured minds in their image, a flood of hailstones
from many assailants, both spirits and sages

while I kindly extend myself a parole by taking pills
The request for substances of a personality flaw matrix
Bears twofold ignorance, like the blind man and the Pharisee
Or tormentor and victim, patient cut down by the other's pride
They even autograph themselves with a christogram
a federal offense here might be favored by the true God

Chambers

Birds, and every other winged creature
glean what they can
Whether from worms in the dirt
or the entire sea of man
The worms cower in multitudes
before the height of their upright plans

Therefore, keeping true to inspiration
the ones who penned and envisioned
in watchtower and in prison
without giving way to death
direct their gaze intently
under this trialsome age
far past Gehenna's turbulence
As a minefield is a place
One dearly dreads to risk
Their feet travel in every direction but the sunrise
As smoke from Rome went deep into the East

There was an inscription meant for all
"Stand firm" it said, in lily gaze text.
But by velocity snared
The ruthless screams of care
By vehemence, by bloodletting,
by sharpness of dead wicked razor
I succumbed before the anatomy of the clouds
(There was a wrongness in the clouds in later days)
Caught up in those clouds, caught up
in the aimlessness of fascinating radiance
I succumbed to the spiraling gate

Behold!
A dark path
where a pyre ends
hellacious and unspeakable
It is the realization of a dubious knowledge
The piecing together of a mosaic
Madness and the burning dragon

The flawed mystery within the night-sky
Finished now towards knowing
Like the resurrection of lizard bones
scattered across every desert
(the roots of suffering go deep)

I have survived, and I will oppose
That aimless ghost, that wanderer
On the road without prayer
Whose gaze of iron eyes are spears
Veritas est ipsa, truth banishes.

Desolation

Sins left me misshapen
Like fragile growth in denying sun and water
roots in between him and me
That tied ragged lungs together, heaving
and caught in the sense of gnashing teeth
living this means dangerously fertile ideas
borne by trees of calamitous thought

On the rampant fields of desolation
Ignorance designs frustrated soils of change
like weeds, now a wasting body
Lorded over by zones of flies
Caught in their static trance
A harmonious drone to the powerful voids
That can no longer bar my weeping

It takes a long time to survive the perils
As creeping maggots burrow in carcass and dirt
smelted and dross and blood-cell batteries
Are able to recharge or refine the heart, as gold.
Against the fight of the internal cries,
I will carry this gifted electrum in a bottle
A remembered tonic for the past severity of growth
That lets little else grow but iron cast error

Precision is needed for exacting self-judgement now
So carvings made with bitumen, to build, to stand it must be
shielded by the cornerstone, as the stars burst pharaonically
In loud breaking all structure of barren "ifs"
Crushing fist to the heirarchy of the powerless
By this exclamation I saw the sun in terrifying heights with myself
And the sea beyond was burning the whole brick city I'd built
Either vision, is ecstatic enough to mean the same thing.

Grief

The meaning in your embrace
Is like fire churning out smoke
As numberless tears
From fumes of inchoate loss
Are destined
To run their course

Opacity-
pharmaceutically hobbled mind

They adjusted lens for transparency and the reversal
(take a pill)
After a decade or so
(take a pill)
There is a certain greyness of eyesight
(take a pill)
A dullness of heart, and muteness
(take a pill)
of speech and hearing. It lets
(take a pill)
very little grow from within
(take a pill)
Lepers have less frustration
(take a pill)
The feel of being an ogre

Take a pill
My liver must be shot

The One Perishing

He meditates on violence
Under the shadow of fear
Leading to luminaries nearer
than sulfurous stars

Making peace with his sin
Is never an option for them
In such human trials conflicting
His heart is bound to fail

But their visceral words
Sound signals coupled to melody
Greatness poured from their lips
Calling full throated down on him
they do not hold back

Bent by one crushing mystery
And a thousand unsown seeds
He fails to be guided by blinding wind
for rejecting heartbeat's unsound din

In his thirst for ice
of original hate
He drowned in the constant mechanisms
of belief in fate

They left behind patterns of compassion,
a foundation to follow of overwrought designs
A forecast on the forsaken horizon
Where the moon, in his majesty
grows wiser.

Witness

Secret grief; like dead thought
Veils the insane lack of truth
Just like vain memory turns
To a second witness lost in the shouts of dust

Ambulance

Within the bowels of the city, clemency
claimed the cornerstone of death
Alive! To pain without rest
Emergency! Sirens misguide the blessed
The dying breath is murky, unclear
Heavens fertilized by thoughts and fears
Growing stars like flowers
Over powerless tears
As the constellations threw down their spears
And the streetlamps burned with agony
at the horizon's heels

Hallways

There is a purpose in restraint
To disallow the teeth of snakes purchase
Nor let one become one with the self.
Motionless clad and disgracefully mad
There followed me patterns
where a theocrat had no surety.
So I allegedly became
an autocrat of various devotion to the insane.
And the autocrat I could not see embittered me
I was imperilled by the sound of the sea.

Far secluded, in the refuge of lea
In the edge of halls they speak, at least three
About veils over distant power
And in lesser degree of manifold signs
Agents clamored around city lines
in the past I would have eaten this terror
But here is where I oppose clandestine error
"I don't want to die" bellowed in my head
Miles reach forward, towards the end
"You must try" the inculcation said
A cold voice whispered of unending dread

Humanity Bound

The tribe of physicians make captives of the breathless
and burn up the golden trusted declarations
that once their patients pretended to memorize
Or pay tribute to their coldest demands

Austerely they direct their cause to increase the dose of pain
Conspiring false light for the dim trial thru to Sunday
Subjected lamps of holy galaxy, and lamps of wicked earth
Wattage, volts and amps measured only for the insanity versed

And it was then among the ruined tongues, under the malevolent moon with
fire
Doctors paralyzed them with a fearsome jargon's choir
Voicelessly their teeth chatter the sudden cold with questions
They are thirsty, so thirsty for ice, the worse it becomes

The doors of rejection opened to the wind-spun ocean
Tragic hints in the foam, the sea remembers to forget
All a complement of lost lodestars, broken compasses, and shipwrecks
And great numbers of fish that churn the milk of the stars

I'm Sorry

I woke, rising, one night,
wandering and weeping
Believing in death, devastation
and designs of grieving
How will we escape this
irredeemable frailty
of hearts, tongues and minds

Under a lamp,
a prism's potential is cast
A beam of many
turning our legacy
into a divisive blessing
colors of love that everlast
Shining in one too many sad smiles

For all of us
Let us become not-that which causes
In terror I have wept
With the glow of the sun decieving
For I remember in daylight dreaming
How the light in her face had died
And the remnant life in her voice had cried

I saw myself for many years before
An endurer of casual torment
And a distant observer now
To the day to day passing of my life
Remembering where certainty tried
unbounded, sunlight, and free
Love in nostalgic memory
I cannot bear the idea of this loss
Let alone a road of cramped life
Im so sorry I could not be
For what I am is not what you see
Forgive me

("Ours is a path
Subject to nothing
But this") - Brian Gianelli

149

Roaring

The lion roars
The aimless wanderer, throwing fragments
Portal sounds wildly, wildly sounds the gong
Wild unkempt gazer ever over anger torn apart

What is the seed of rebellion?
Is it lingering doubt?
Oblique, inchoate refusal? Peril?
Aimless voice? Or slanderous thought?
Throwing pot-shots at divine nature?
What then am I, am I one who carries this?
How do I defeat it?

Purpose

When up, below, the cradles turn
They pan before the strong, who countenanced
Like silver sky, silver rain, and gold fields burned,
Blast horns to love's glory, tossed by morning lights

Hungry storms prowl, before the baneful
unbearable feelings of exhuming,
lying tears. For thoughts unfaithful,
hope's great horizons shift weight's bearing

I feel like I'm at war, my thoughts travailed
By my past, purposed by my sighs, aligned
To times of gentle myth, words once learned, now failed
Under select and wicked, long-lasting crimes

Like sad eyes noticed clinking music coins
I will waver, near the storm, bound and joined.

The Flies of Gehenna

I know God is above all corruption
And with the substance broken inside me
(More than once) – came masks of many teeming
despoilers. In what choice life remains
I burden the fear I may, with many, never dream again.

A knowing field, weeds and wheat, sparked to the true
Still every carefully thought out immediacy
Fails - who other but I am at fault
I will drop my shield in this ultimatum
On this sickbed droned by flies

The substance was hope, and I imagined too much

Devouring

As waters underground for the thirsting
A merciless sign blotting the sun with sin,
Arose pain, fingers of evil and all surrendered sanctity
There is no end to the grottoed fountains din.

What was cast down is crushed
To bend by the lawful hand.
Out of shards of misery I began to rebuild
A mosaic to cover the trespassed land.

Which devouring omen leads to verity?
Here in my warm and lusterless palm
I seek any aid to a truth that must be burned
Like an agate's dull fire of lonely, lettered song.

This was my gauntlet before and beyond me
My mind crashing down around the insult
One glanced birth of the true stone and cloud
Forged by God forever.

The Peril

Voiceless do I watch alone
with the darkling thrush and spritely sparrow
A hope that never answered the weeping
With anything save eternity's traces
And the golden egg and pupil of the sun
searched unsparingly for flames on the earth undone
A symmetry of fault in the nimbus hatched
Between two, tranquil restraint of veins that also shine
With subtle green blood, a proud old voice
Shouting through the skin cells of my furnace
And the hammer of unreason's anvil, hot
Clamored in soundless snowflake patterns churning the air
in the iron grip of true despair

And I stood before this wilderness in a season
Where the bright gold trees whispered
Of all our forged, hosted human frailties
Telling of crimes and failed woven paths
That play the telling traveling chords
of clock-like wandering, birds and criminals.
A music that is cold and aching, in any season
So that I obey the height of boldness
within the true uncountable sky
For I am never hungry, and sleepless, and on fire
With a mind that steals notes, struck
by omens in truth answered and revealed

I am always sorry, for I never
answered our connections with anything but fire

Crosses

inspired by subjective look at Falun Gong

The Father saw the embryo
Of every enemy in man
Like arrows toward the sun
Cathedral gong sounds the moon, laying vengeance
On the desperate disregard kept in urns
There in the grottoes of New York City

Vision to the coalition at the center of the earth
Disciples of Eastern esotericism chitter and croak
Same cross as the West, new spokes
Pro-creators and preachers of the same chaos
at the heart of the transgression
Railway spears thru the graveyard, comets streaking above
Visiting their dust upon the center of the earth

and under a boiling black tempest
Idol heaps stand and idle clicking of hooves sound
Who among them was taught like Faust?
One day they will collapse inwardly with no rescue
From their notable notions for survival of this horror
The city will never sleep, outstretched arms
feed in spirit junk food plenitudes

A taste of the macabre, a task for the insane
The threats are real, don't ask me today
I am flying on wings of peril, wonder and names
Decisively caught up in the amazement of it all.
My shrieking eyes for the end are met
with caroling ignorance by others

Boiling, black eyed hateful skies
There is simplicity in true hatred
Tears still sunder me, sending up smoke
a signal fire – Double, double churn and toil
An attempt to capture that vital essence
Strength by stanza, influence by line
Or burn this page.

Tides

A Pindaric Ode

What should I say about the worst days of my life?
What cloud conveyed the image
What mirrors were privy shown?
What bird heard the sound
What music could sign the road?
What watcher could surmise it
Whose torment was it anyway?

I have become just a casual observer deprived
To the day to day passing
Of life with all its sense void
Anger and aged disbelief
Lungs much like vents hot with grief
Choke on bitter, beautiful air
Like light in a prism or the rain
Like the glow in a beloved womanly eye

Certain crystalline ending page of the eternal
Burned me inside out like a supernova
And driven mad by pain, I picked up a pen
Tables concealed behind the chemical prison walls
Finding no sleep, no rest, no haven marked safe
I spilled the inkwell over my heart, then and now
Some agency in blood wrote the end of all their days
I have no love left for anyone today
So I turn off all these channels
Just to keep one more fingerprint on sane
Last of all I turn off
my dull and misty shame.

From the author:
an excerpt from
a Work in Progress

"Couriant and the Waking"
working title

Coming soon

The cathedral was towering, conspiratorially shadowed in the dying sunlight. Before the pass in the mountains, behind the gates leading to the town they found the trail of the royal retinue, just as the angel had guided him. They left their horses with the stablemaster at the inn. They passed a marching line of monks, mumbling chants, led by one carrying an incense prayer burner, all with black and brown hoods. And through the labyrinthine woods Couriant spearheaded them to the camp, his eyes still led by the white mercy and golden sash.

It was clear they had sought not to seek attention to themselves, should they be known. When the King emerged from his tent he had no crown, no royal garment. A simple peddlers cloak and brown and gold raiment. For the townsfolk here none would have guessed their visitor's identity. Only Couriant and his men would have recognized them.

He waved his guards off and approached Couriant with a gait of humble power, and there was a commoner's glint in his eye; like the surefooted longing for hewn stone or harvested wheat. Ethereally, the guards directed Couriant's own retinue into their camps and the man who was King took his own to usher him along before the mountain pass. He gave a few simple commands of quiet and assuagement to Sabir and they parted. His men were uneasy but obedient.

He knew not to address him with any terms at all but rather to wait until he was spoken to. There was a chill silence, and the hawks circled, rooting crows from their hiding places. The mountains were dark and morbid before the pass as the King, his guards and Couriant climbed the hill and gazed East. Against the mountains in the backdrop, towards the holy city somewhere past the horizon.

After a long moment he heaved in a heavy breath and exhaled. The mist was like a conflagration. The King is still breathing. This would have calmed many anxious hearts. The horizon gleamed dimly for them, the glow of far off burning cities. In certainty, it must for now be a peaceful fire.

"I knew you would come, Couriant. In fact, I commanded it."

There was a heavy, burdened sense of grief and anxiety. Couriant looked at the smoke from the campfires behind them with frail, changing eyes. The meaty smoke of the burning seer. How undue an obscenity for a man to be like smoked salmon. A polymath nightmare, vivid in reflexive threats and curses, the smoke then lingered in the air hallucinatorily. His own breath was meager before him, a pallid undeserving sustenance to a body culled by the sin of that same unknown. A terrible remembrance, and Rylian's was even darker. He remained silent, and heavily the King strained his gaze.

"Accordingly, the oak tree under the westering clouds at the fork in the road has lived a century longer than anything else here alive in sight. And I have been reading the old scrolls, my friend. Do you know what they say of our plight?"

He turned his face to a sudden wind with closed, harrowed grey browed eyes, and there was a hawk passing high up against a cloud. The only cloud in the sky, a simple tuft, almost like an imaginative decor. Couriant looked away with a collapsing distance in his own eyes. He wanted to ask about Nalia's purpose and safety, but obeyed the force of will next to him. An attentive ear, an invocation perhaps. A telling glint in his voice of starlight born for other worlds. The Cathedral must be a brewery atop the cliffs, for ailments as well as alcohol. Borrowed time by lord's blood. The royal crest flashed vividly in that patch of the sky the hawk had crossed, and refracted here in their own shadows at their feet, shining darkly, secretively. Skinny light from corroded doors.

"From the ziggurats, formed by man, smoke trails float before the moon, an affront to that luminary. Making new the spikes of the stars and shining their memorial about the grains of sand by the sea. There are thoughts of constellations in the yearning, reaching tips of grass at the oak's feet, their king, who thinks not to yearn for celestial knowing nor divine blessing found nowhere on earth. He knows only the sun.'

'The incense fires of our great city offer up man's similitudiness entreaties. Proud oak, tall king; subtle grasses, able subjects; bitter slaves, and final offerings: one collusion, ceased."

He glanced at Couriant sidelong, his robust body firm and unchangeable, like a standing stone or an unhewn rockface.

"Armies of stars and sand conspire together to make all these things we see whole and unified. One unseen unity in all of it, perhaps that leaf or this glimmer or that blade.

He gestured serenely, like a priest or potentate, a knowing voice; leaf, grass, his sword.

'One day, in the temple, I found a broken clay cup. It was swept up by an attendant and cast into the trashpits over the southern wall. One day, complete. One day.'

One day, Couriant, the city and the Kingdom will suffer the same shattering amidst all this indifferent, calamitous yearning. Hope, despair, why should we speak in such clear diction? To speak in endless garbled tongues of uncertainty instead..." he gazed long at Couriant for the first time. His eyes were heavy with burden, gray irises of trapped insistence. "That is what a king hopes for, my adjutant. The kind of causality that leads to forbidden knowledge from endless natural cycles of aphorisms.'

But, rely on something overhead for now, higher. Two eyes, one heart, an attentive ear. Your own place is in the grave. That is what my councilor would say."

He laughed, and the sound was a bark and a shout. The ravens in the trees before the mountains cried out and took flight. They watched them flee together with a distant sense of their own power. Men and beast cower, tremble, and crumble.

"Tell me Couriant," the King said patronizingly, a hint of vigor in his rich voice. "Were you ever a sailor?"

He paused and tasted the substance with his mind. A drink of subterfuge, or a rhetorical method? He answered after a brief pause.

"I sailed for merchants guilds before the guard. As young as I was I can remember dreaming of building boats and braving the seas. I've trained as first mate on a vessel for your navy, I can read the stars. I know the truth about the Great Divide. If I could go back...well, frankly it was my first calling. But I would not change my course, not for the brightest and most fortuitous star."

The King rumbled deep in his chest. It was a chuckling adornment, a pleased laughter. He looked towards the partitioned forest, where the oak was at the cleft in the road. A feast in the Abbey, from the smell and the smoke and the murmurs. Where Couriant and his men had first trembled upon the scene before the Cathedral's rise. A ley lode, a place of power, perhaps. Royal eyes will seek and find.

"The truth, you say...

It's threat has been like that clay cup I saw, Couriant; shattered and cast into the pit. A conspiracy, nothing more; no sure hand to thwart it within my own demesne, no clear mind to see. A conspiracy, a shadow fable to teach our powers to fear the uprisen candles in the hands of revolters becoming the conflagration. Nothing more. A clay cup we do not even regard. One day complete. It is with God that all days sustain to their finish.

'The Guard, your men, they are different. They teach legends as historical values, in their own telling. Their love for King driving them to secrete themselves even from me, from my daughter. The last serpentine tooth we desire for protection in their own solution of venom. '

Tell me, Couriant, what do you know about the Black Hand?"

He snailed his gaze upon the King's unshod feet, handled only by fine sandals, like a prophet, strangely incongruous, and raised his gaze upwards, as if to heaven, to meet Rylian's certain, unknowing eyes. A portal to fear and love, a designation for the mastery over animalistic things, of ferocity in a hand taught to command for service. The humanity. The head of the millions. He looked at him in his solemn, craglike face,

160

without knowing, without seeing, and said absently:

"Fables, myths. Aphorisms. Just parables to teach the guard. Courage, honor, power. That's all they've ever been."

King Rylian turned abruptly and began to walk down the rise facing west towards his tents. A terse lapse of speech and encouragement, as if he had expected something more. The guards followed behind them, and the leaves whispered simpler inanities from a bitter wind before the sparsely decorated interruptions of Rylian's commanding voice.

"No, Couriant. Archran is nothing but a tool. The Black Hand is rising. They are coming. And we do not have the might nor the insight to resist them, this time."

"The enemy lurks in scattered messages in city alleyways, routes and passes in the mountains, and sparsely guarded caravan merchants. Among shrines and hostels, and bleak taverns for drifters. Some in my own echelons believe in the existence of spies and usurpers even in the royal court. It is delicate. They do not know the sea. There is something about the sanctity of water."

They entered his tent in silence, a shock of air about him like electric tendrils thrumming for his heart and thought and brain. He was breathing sharply now, and black mandala patterns danced before his eyes on the King's patterned raiment. It was royal, he saw. Even here, Rylian would declare his distinction, albeit unknowing. The glyphs and runes of royal lineage in faint filigree of gold and some other metal; no crests, but a subtle choice of garment to berth them from us.

"You will be our vanguard, Couriant, as ever. I have been given a purpose for you that I must implore you."

He pored over the old maps on the oak table in the royal tent, sending his guards outside. Couriant recognized many of them. Kingdom maps, some of outlying islands, old borders. King Rylian took one other from the bookshelf and sprawled it out with both hands, calloused and worn with ringed fingers. Esoteric brotherhoods and seals of lineage in gold and ruby and silver, ancient in their own days.

"Vile vortices..." he murmured, and Couriant nodded at the mystery. It was a map of landless oceans, designed from prophecy and seers. "I asked you, what facts you knew of the Black Hand...but in fact..." he waved his hand majestically at the maps.

He gazed at Couriant with a mystique, an air of implication, designing to see what was in his heart. Then he looked back down at the map and placed one finger on a point in the Ocean marked by unreadable runes. A stab of lightning or a fire dart. He was looming over the table like a mountain above a holy site.

"It is here, in the rising, trapless door, Couriant. The place of uncharacteristic strength."

His voice was dark, portentous. Couriant mustered himself with a hand unwittingly on

161

his sword hilt. It was the place of the vile vortices. The great expanse that older times had thought was the edge of the world where all the waters spill off the edge into the void. A legend that spoke of tribal dooms and men with hooks for teeth, monsters of nightmares. Great wars and the Great Divide. A long attenuated story of battles and the mysterious power of God. Racial conflicts before the Kingdom with savagely constellatory boundaries.

"I will go wherever you send me," he said simply. His voice was cutting in the thickened air, tremulous like newly rung steel. His sword remained still and hostile in it's scabbard. It was an affirmation, a seal. The guard's honor. The King spoke again after a long crippling pause, staring into him with a merciless appraisal. He felt heat in his hands and neck.

"We know midheaven. You must as the vanguard search beyond the waters below, beyond hearing of our people's grieving outcries. Like women weeping and sober for their dying sons.'

'The Black Hand...I believe they seek the same thing. The people of this fable. We know they are as real as us. I want you to find them first. Nevermind the name of their land or their gods. The clouds will part for us in eternity, one day. The stars will breathe again a simpler breath. A blade of grass cut by a sword. Glass that breaks upon the bricks."

Couriant looked at him with questions in his eyes. "My Lord?"

He was staring at the map with beetle like intensity. An eagle's prayer. "We have never seen it. No one has. Thus your quest is all the more integral.'

I have a boat for you where the Kingdom's reach is still intact. The boat was crafted with my own mind in it's timbers. We will be with you on your trials. My daughter is about your neck."

Startled, Couriant raised a hand to the pendant underneath his shirt. It was humming vapidly in his own veins. Their eyes were everywhere, like stars or clouds or birds.

"She is quite safe. It was her intellect that brought us this far. She will be a greater queen than I am a sire. Your entourage must remain behind. They love her, don't they? Have they learned to know their service as full as you have, adjutant?"

His guards entered at a silent command Couriant could not see. Rylian gave him the select maps, rolled and bound in copper tubes. He reminded him of the lodestars, but Couriant was already affixed to the affrontery, the knowledge sure, the reason scarce. They saw him out and Rylian spoke entreatingly after him, a severity to the rhythm and tone of his voice:

"The wind chases after wind. Water flows with water. Become water, listen for the wind. We believe in you, Couriant. No one else must know of it."

162

"Skrivener carried the last host loyal to me within a keep nearest the ocean. Make for it before departing. They will know you by my prow, and perhaps some by the gift of my daughter. However, keep it secret, if you can. To contain forceful intricacies is no delicate gift. But I can see; you have the strength for my faith. I would send no other. And pride bears down upon calling you a son-in-law when you return."

You are not fleeing, Couriant; we will not sever you. We seek the answers, and a victory, with them. I do not know if you will die. Without them, we all will."

The eyes of thousands he had never believed in turned upon him. A prophet or an imagination? He left, ushered out, with a dazzling perplexity and a voiceless throat. A throat of dungeon thirst. Sending one man to sail the ocean seeking after a fable, a dream, as the means to preserve the Kingdom...it felt like the King had hammered the last nail of hope into his own palms.

The guards left him at the pass turning upon the oak. He gazed at it's gently rustling leaves, it's great garrulous branches, like the King's voice, garrulous and strong, the Cathedral looming as a black presence before each gaze of the land, centuries of toil in the dirt, of growth and growth of understanding. His eyes full of the kingship of both, crowned branches and stars turning, burning in their hair. And he turned south upon the road back to the inn and where his four final loyal warriors remained to be handed over. For a cause he could not now understand.

Manufactured by Amazon.ca
Bolton, ON